Model Speeches for Practise

by Grenville Kleiser

PREFACE

This book contains a varied representation of successful speeches by eminently successful speakers. They furnish, in convenient form, useful material for study and practise.

The student is earnestly recommended to select one speech at a time, analyze it carefully, note its special features, practise it aloud, and then proceed to another. In this way he will cover the principal forms of public speaking, and enable himself to apply his knowledge to any occasion.

The cardinal rule is that a speaker learns to speak by speaking, hence a careful reading and study of these speeches will do much to develop the student's taste for correct literary and oratorical form.

GRENVILLE KLEISER. New York City, August, 1919.

CONTENTS

INTRODUCTION

AIMS AND PURPOSES OF SPEAKING

It is obvious that the style of your public speaking will depend upon the specific purpose you have in view. If you have important truths which you wish to make known, or a great and definite cause to serve, you are likely to speak about it with earnestness and probably with eloquence.

If, however, your purpose in speaking is a selfish one--if your object is self-exploitation, or to serve some special interest of your own--if you regard your speaking as an irksome task, or are unduly anxious as to what your hearers will think of you and your effort--then you are almost sure to fail.

On the other hand, if you have the interests of your hearers sincerely at heart--if you really wish to render a worthy public service--if you lose all thought of self in your heartfelt desire to serve others--then you will have the most essential requirements of true and enduring oratory.

THE NECESSITY OF A DEFINITE OBJECT

It is of the highest importance for you to have in mind a clear conception of the end you wish to achieve by your speaking. This purpose should characterize all you say, so that at each step in your speech you will feel sure of making steady progress toward the desired object.

As a public speaker you assume serious responsibility. You are to influence men for weal or woe. The words you speak are like so many seeds, planted in the minds of your hearers, there to grow and multiply according to their kind. What you say may have far-reaching effects, hence the importance of careful forethought in the planning and preparation of your speeches.

The highest aim of your public speaking is not merely to instruct or entertain, but to influence the wills of men, to make men think as you think, and to persuade them to act in the manner you desire. This is a lofty aim, when supported by a good cause, and worthy of your greatest talents and efforts.

THE KEY TO SUCCESS IN SPEAKING

The key to greatness of speech is sincerity. You must yourself be so thoroughly imbued with the truth and desirability of what you are urging upon others that they will be imprest by your integrity of purpose. To have their confidence and good will is almost to win your cause.

But you must have deep and well-grounded convictions before you can hope to convince and influence other men. Duty, necessity, magnanimity, innate conviction, and sincere interest in the welfare of others,--these beget true fervor and are essential to passionate and persuasive speaking.

Lord Lytton emphasized the vital importance of earnest purpose in the speaker. Referring to speech in the British Parliament he said, "Have but fair sense and a competent knowledge of your subject, and then be thoroughly in earnest to impress your own honest conviction upon others, and no matter what your delivery, tho your gestures shock every rule in Quintilian, you will command the ear and influence the debates of the most accomplished, the most fastidious, and, take it altogether, the noblest assembly of freemen in the world."

Keep in mind that the purpose of your public speaking is not only to convince but also to persuade your hearers. It is not sufficient that they merely agree with what you say; you must persuade them also to act as you desire.

Hence you should aim to reach both their minds and hearts. Solid argument, clear method, and indisputable facts are necessary for the first purpose; vivid imagination, concrete illustration, and animated feeling are necessary for the second.

THE NEED OF A KNOWLEDGE OF HUMAN NATURE

It will be of great practical value to you to have a knowledge of the average man comprising your audience, his tastes, preferences, prejudices, and proclivities. The more you adapt your speech to such an average man, the more successful are you likely to be in influencing the entire audience.

Aim, therefore, to use words, phrases, illustrations, and arguments such as you think the average man will readily understand. Avoid anything which would cause confusion, distraction, or prejudice in his mind. Use every reasonable means to win his good will and approval.

Your speech is not a monolog, but a dialog, in which you are the speaker, and the auditor a silent tho questioning listener. His mind is in a constant attitude of interrogation toward you. And upon the degree of your success in answering such silent but insistent questions will depend the ultimate success of your speaking.

The process of persuading the hearer depends chiefly upon first being persuaded yourself. You may be devoid of feeling, and yet convince your hearers; but to reach their hearts and to move them surely toward the desired purpose, you must yourself be moved.

Your work as a public speaker is radically different from that of the actor or reciter. You are not impersonating some one else, nor interpreting the thought of another. You must above all things be natural, real, sincere and earnest. Your work is creative and constructive.

THE RIGHT ATTITUDE OF A SPEAKER

However much you may study, plan, or premeditate, there must be no indication of conscious or studied attempt in the act of speaking to an audience. At that time everything must be merged into your personality.

Your earnestness in speaking arises principally from having a distinct conception of the object aimed at and a strong desire to accomplish it. Under these circumstances you summon to your aid all your available power of thought and feeling. Your mental faculties are stimulated into their fullest activity, and you bend every effort toward the purpose before you.

But however zealous you may feel about the truth or righteousness of the cause you espouse, you will do well always to keep within the bounds of moderation. You can be vigorous without violence, and enthusiastic without extravagance.

You must not only thoroughly know yourself and your subject, but also your audience. You should carefully consider the best way to bring them and yourself into unity. You may do this by making an appeal to some principle commonly recognized and approved by men, such as patriotism, justice, humanity, courage, duty, or righteousness.

What Phillips Brooks said about the preacher, applies with equal truth to other forms of public speaking:

"Whatever is in the sermon must be in the preacher first; clearness, logicalness, vivacity, earnestness, sweetness, and light, must be personal qualities in him before they are qualities of thought and language in what he utters to his people."

After you have earnestly studied the principles of public speaking you should plan to have regular and frequent practise in addressing actual audiences. There are associations and societies everywhere, constantly in quest of good speakers. There will be ample opportunities for you if you have properly developed your speaking abilities.

And now to sum up some of the most essential things for you:

1. READ ALOUD EVERY DAY

This is indispensable to your greatest progress in speech culture. Reading aloud, properly done, compels you to pronounce the words, instead of skimming over them as in silent reading. It gives you the additional benefit of receiving a vocal impression of the rhythm and structure of the composition.

Keep in mind the following purposes of your reading aloud:

1. To improve your speaking voice.

2. To acquire distinct enunciation.

3. To cultivate correct pronunciation.

4. To develop English style.

5. To increase your stock of words.

6. To store your memory with facts.

7. To analyze an author's thoughts.

8. To broaden your general knowledge.

2. FORM THE NOTE-BOOK HABIT

Keep separate note-books for the subjects in which you are deeply interested and on which you intend some time to speak in public. Write in them promptly any valuable ideas which come to you from the four principal sources--observation, conversation, reading, and meditation.

You will be surprized to find how rapidly you can acquire useful data in this way. In an emergency you can turn to the speech-material you have accumulated and quickly solve the problem of "what to say."

Keep the contents of your note-books in systematic order. Classify ideas under distinct headings. When possible write the ideas down in regular speech form. Once a week read aloud the contents of your note-books.

3. DAILY STUDY YOUR DICTIONARY

Read aloud each day from your dictionary for at least five minutes, and give special attention to the pronunciation and meaning of words. This is one of the most useful exercises for building a large vocabulary.

Develop the dictionary habit. Be interested in words. Study them in their contexts. Make special lists of your own. Select special words for special uses. Note significant words in your general reading.

Think of words as important tools for public speaking. Choose them with discrimination in your daily conversation. Consult your dictionary for the meanings of words about which you are in doubt. Be an earnest student of words.

4. SYSTEMATICALLY DEVELOP YOUR MENTAL POWERS

Give some time each day to the development of a judicial mind. Learn to think deliberately and carefully. Study causes and principles. Look deeply into things.

Be impartial in your examination of a subject. Study all sides of a question or problem. Weigh the evidence with the purpose of ascertaining the truth.

Beware the peril of prejudice. Keep your mind wide open to receive the facts. Look at a subject from the other man's viewpoint. Cultivate breadth of mind. Do not let your personal interests or desires mislead you. Insist upon securing the truth at all costs.

5. DAILY PRACTISE COMPOSITION

Frequent use of the pen is essential to proficiency in speaking. Write a little every day to form your English style. Daily exercise in writing will rapidly develop felicity and fluency of speech.

Test your important ideas by putting them into writing. Constantly cultivate clearness of expression. Examine, criticize, and improve your own compositions.

Copy in your handwriting at least a page daily from one of the great English stylists. Continue this exercise for a month and note the improvement in your speech and writing.

6. PRACTISE IMPROMPTU SPEAKING

At least once a day stand up, in the privacy of your room, and make an impromptu speech of two or three minutes. Select any subject which interests you. Aim at fluency of style rather than depth of thought.

In these daily efforts, use the best chest voice at your command, enunciate clearly, open your mouth well, and imagine yourself addressing an actual audience. A month's regular practise of this exercise will convince you of its great value.

7. STUDY SUCCESSFUL PUBLIC SPEAKERS

Hear the best public speakers available to you. Observe them critically. Ask yourself such questions as these:

1. How does this speaker impress me?

2. Does he proceed in the most effective manner possible?

3. Does he convince me of the truth of his statements?

4. Does he persuade me to act as he wishes?

5. What are the elements of success in this speaker?

As you faithfully apply these various suggestions, you will constantly improve in the art of public speaking, and so learn to wield this mighty power not simply for your personal gratification but for the inspiration and betterment of your fellow men.

MODEL SPEECHES FOR PRACTISE

AFTER-DINNER SPEAKING

BY JAMES RUSSELL LOWELL

My Lord Coleridge, My Lords, Ladies and Gentlemen:--I confess that my mind was a little relieved when I found that the toast to which I am to respond rolled three gentlemen, Cerberus-like into one, and when I saw Science pulling impatiently at the leash on my left, and Art on my right, and that therefore the responsibility of only a third part of the acknowledgment has fallen to me. You, my lord, have alluded to the difficulties of after-dinner oratory. I must say that I am one of those who feel them more keenly the more after-dinner speeches I make. There are a great many difficulties in the way, and there are three principal ones, I think. The first is having too much to say, so that the words, hurrying to escape, bear down and trample out the life of each other. The second is when, having nothing to say, we are expected to fill a void in the minds of our hearers. And I think the third, and most formidable, is the necessity of following a speaker who is sure to say all the things you meant to say, and better than you, so that we are tempted to exclaim, with the old grammarian, "Hang these fellows, who have said all our good things before us!"

Now the Fourth of July has several times been alluded to, and I believe it is generally thought that on that anniversary the spirit of a certain bird known to heraldic ornithologists--and I believe to them alone--as the spread eagle, enters into every American's breast, and compels him, whether he will or no, to pour forth a flood of national self-laudation. This, I say, is the general superstition, and I hope that a few words of mine may serve in some sort to correct it. I ask you, if there is any other people who have confined their national self-laudation to one day in the year. I may be allowed to make one remark as a personal experience. Fortune had willed it that I should see as many--perhaps more--cities and manners of men as Ulysses; and I have observed one general fact, and that is, that the adjectival epithet which is prefixt to all the virtues is invariably the epithet which geographically describes the country that I am in. For instance, not to take any real name, if I am in the kingdom of Lilliput, I hear of the Lilliputian virtues. I hear courage, I hear common sense, and I hear political wisdom called by that name. If I cross to the neighboring Republic Blefusca--for since Swift's time it has become a Republic--I hear all these virtues suddenly qualified as Blefuscan.

I am very glad to be able to thank Lord Coleridge for having, I believe for the first time, coupled the name of the President of the United States with that of her Majesty on an occasion like this. I was struck, both in what he said, and in what our distinguished guest of the evening said, with the frequent recurrence of an adjective which is comparatively new--I mean the word "English-speaking." We continually hear nowadays of the "English-speaking race," of the "English-speaking population." I think this implies, not that we are to forget, not that it would be well for us to forget, that national emulation and that national pride which is implied in the words "Englishman" and "American," but the word implies that there are certain perennial and abiding sympathies between all men of a common descent and a common language. I am sure, my lord, that all you said with regard to the welcome which our distinguished guest will receive in America is true. His eminent talents as an orator, the dignified--I may say the illustrious--manner in which he has sustained the traditions of that succession of great actors who, from the time of Burbage to his own, have illustrated the English stage, will be as highly appreciated there as here.

And I am sure that I may also say that the chief magistrate of England will be welcomed by the bar of the United States, of which I am an unworthy member, and perhaps will be all the more warmly welcomed that he does not come among them to practise. He will find American law administered--and I think he will agree with me in saying ably administered--by judges who, I am sorry to say, sit without the traditional wig of England. I have heard since I came here friends of mine gravely lament this as something prophetic of the decay which was sure to follow so serious an innovation. I answered with a little story which I remember having heard from my father. He remembered the last clergyman in New England who still continued to wear the wig. At first it became a singularity and at last a monstrosity; and the good doctor concluded to leave it off. But there was one poor woman among his parishioners who lamented this sadly, and waylaying the clergyman as he came out of church she said, "Oh, dear doctor, I have always listened to your sermon with the greatest edification and comfort, but now that the wig is gone all is gone." I have thought I have seen some signs of encouragement in the faces of my English friends after I have consoled them with this little story.

But I must not allow myself to indulge in any further remarks. There is one virtue, I am sure, in after-dinner oratory, and that is brevity; and as to that I am reminded of a story. The Lord Chief Justice has told you what are the ingredients of after-dinner oratory. They are the joke, the quotation, and the platitude; and the successful platitude, in my judgment, requires a very high order of genius. I believe that I have not given you a quotation, but I am reminded of something which I heard when very young--the story of a Methodist clergyman in America. He was preaching at a camp meeting, and he was preaching upon the miracle of Joshua, and he began his sermon with this sentence: "My hearers, there are three motions of the sun. The first is the straightforward or direct motion of the sun; the second is the retrograde or backward motion of the sun; and the third is the motion mentioned in our text--'the sun stood still.'"

Now, gentlemen, I don't know whether you see the application of the story-- I hope you do. The after-dinner orator at first begins and goes straight forward--that is the straightforward motion of the sun. Next he goes back and begins to repeat himself--that is the backward motion of the sun. At last he has the good sense to bring himself to the end, and that is the motion mentioned in our text, as the sun stood still.

ENGLAND, MOTHER OF NATIONS

BY RALPH WALDO EMERSON

Mr. Chairman and Gentlemen:--It is pleasant to me to meet this great and brilliant company, and doubly pleasant to see the faces of so many distinguished persons on this platform. But I have known all these persons already. When I was at home, they were as near to me as they are to you. The arguments of the League and its leader are known to all friends of free trade. The gaieties and genius, the political, the social, the parietal wit of "Punch" go duly every fortnight to every boy and girl in Boston and New York. Sir, when I came to sea, I found the "History of Europe" on the ship's cabin table, the property of the captain;--a sort of program or play-bill to tell the seafaring New Englander what he shall find on landing here. And as for Dombey, sir, there is no land where paper exists to print on, where it is not found; no man who can read, that does not read it, and, if he can not, he finds some charitable pair of eyes that can, and hears it.

But these things are not for me to say; these compliments tho true, would better come from one who felt and understood these merits more. I am not here to exchange civilities with you, but rather to speak on that which I am sure interests these gentlemen more than their own praises; of that which is good in holidays and working-days, the same in one century and in another century. That which lures a solitary American in the woods with the wish to see England, is the moral peculiarity of the Saxon race,--its commanding sense of right and wrong,--the love and devotion to that,--this is the imperial trait, which arms them with the scepter of the globe. It is this which lies at the foundation of that aristocratic character, which certainly wanders into strange vagaries, so that its origin is often lost sight of, but which, if it should lose this, would find itself paralyzed; and in trade, and in the mechanic's shop, gives that honesty in performance, that thoroughness and solidity of work, which is a national characteristic. This conscience is one element, and the other is that loyal adhesion, that habit of friendship, that homage of man to man, running through all classes,--the electing of worthy persons to a certain fraternity, to acts of kindness and warm and staunch support, from year to year, from youth to age,--which is alike lovely and honorable to those who render and those who receive it;--which stands in strong contrast with the superficial attachments of other races, their excessive courtesy, and short-lived connection.

You will think me very pedantic, gentlemen, but holiday tho it be, I have not the smallest interest in any holiday, except as it celebrates real and not pretended joys; and I think it just, in this time of gloom and commercial disaster, of affliction and beggary in these districts, that on these very accounts I speak of, you should not fail to keep your literary anniversary. I seem to hear you say that, for all that is come and gone, yet we will not reduce by one chaplet or one oak-leaf the braveries of our annual feast. For I must tell you, I was given to understand in my childhood that the British island, from which my forefathers came, was no lotus-garden, no paradise of serene sky and roses and music and merriment all the year round, no, but a cold, foggy, mournful country, where nothing grew well in the open air, but robust men and virtuous women and these of a wonderful fiber and endurance; that their best parts were slowly revealed; their virtues did not come out until they quarrelled; they did not strike twelve the first time; good lovers, good haters, and you could know little about them till you had seen them long, and little good of them till you had seen them in action; that in prosperity they were moody and dumpish, but in adversity they were grand.

Is it not true, sir, that the wise ancients did not praise the ship parting with flying colors from the port, but only that brave sailor which came back with torn sheets and battered sides, stript of her banners, but having ridden out the storm? And so, gentlemen, I feel in regard to this aged England, with the possessions, honors and trophies, and also with the infirmities of a thousand years gathering around her, irretrievably committed as she now is to many old customs which can not be suddenly changed; pressed upon by the transitions of trade, and new and all incalculable modes, fabrics, arts, machines and competing populations,--I see her not dispirited, not weak, but well remembering that she has seen dark days before; indeed with a kind of instinct that she sees a little better in a cloudy day, and that in storm of battle and calamity, she has a secret vigor and a pulse like a cannon. I see her in her old age, not decrepit, but young, and still daring to believe in her power of endurance and expansion. Seeing this, I say, All hail! mother of nations, mother of heroes, with strength still equal to the time; still wise to entertain and swift to execute the policy which the mind and heart of mankind require in the present hour, and thus only hospitable to the foreigner, and truly a home to the thoughtful and generous who are born in the soil. So be it! so be it! If it be not so, if the courage of England goes with the chances of a commercial crisis, I will go back to the capes of Massachusetts, and my own Indian stream, and say to my countrymen, the old race are all gone and the elasticity and hope of mankind must henceforth remain on the Alleghany ranges, or nowhere.

THE AGE OF RESEARCH

BY WILLIAM EWART GLADSTONE

Mr. Chairman, Your Royal Highness, My Lords and Gentlemen:--I think no question can be raised as to the just claims of literature to stand upon the list of toasts at the Royal Academy, and the sentiment is one to which, upon any one of the numerous occasions of my attendance at your hospitable board, I have always listened with the greatest satisfaction until the present day arrived, when I am bound to say that that satisfaction is extremely qualified by the arrangement less felicitous, I think, than any which preceded it that refers to me the duty of returning thanks for Literature. However, obedience is the principle upon which we must proceed, and I have at least the qualification for discharging the duty you have been pleased to place in my hands--that no one has a deeper or more profound sense of the vital importance of the active and constant cultivation of letters as an essential condition of real progress and of the happiness of mankind, and here every one at once perceives that that sisterhood of which the poet spoke, whom you have quoted, is a real sisterhood, for literature and art are alike the votaries of beauty. Of these votaries I may thankfully say that as regards art I trace around me no signs of decay, and none in that estimation in which the Academy is held, unless to be sure, in the circumstance of your poverty of choice of one to reply to this toast.

During the present century the artists of this country have gallantly and nobly endeavored to maintain and to elevate their standard, and have not perhaps in that great task always received that assistance which could be desired from the public taste which prevails around them. But no one can examine even superficially the works which adorn these walls without perceiving that British art retains all its fertility of invention, and this year as much as in any year that I can remember, exhibits in the department of landscape, that fundamental condition of all excellence, intimate and profound sympathy with nature.

As regards literature one who is now beginning at any rate to descend the hill of life naturally looks backward as well as forward, and we must be becoming conscious that the early part of this century has witnessed in this and other countries what will be remembered in future times as a splendid literary age. The elder among us have lived in the lifetime of many great men who have passed to their rest--the younger have heard them familiarly spoken of and still have their works in their hands as I trust they will continue to be in the hands of all generations. I am afraid we can not hope for literature--it would be contrary to all the experience of former times were we to hope that it should be equally sustained at that extraordinarily high level which belongs, speaking roughly, to the first fifty years after the peace of 1815. That was a great period--a great period in England, a great period in Germany, a great period in France, and a great period, too, in Italy.

As I have said, I think we can hardly hope that it should continue on a perfect level at so high an elevation. Undoubtedly the cultivation of literature will ever be dear to the people of this country; but we must remember what is literature and what is not. In the first place we should be all agreed that bookmaking is not literature. The business of bookmaking I have no doubt may thrive and will be continued upon a constantly extending scale from year to year. But that we may put aside. For my own part if I am to look a little forward, what I anticipate for the remainder of the century is an age not so much of literature proper--not so much of great, permanent and splendid additions to those works in which beauty is embodied as an essential condition of production, but rather look forward to an age of research. This is an age of great research--of great research in science, great research in history--an age of research in all the branches of inquiry that throw light upon the former condition whether of our race, or of the world which it inhabits; and it may be hoped that, even if the remaining years of the century be not so brilliant as some of its former periods, in the production of works great in themselves, and immortal,--still they may add largely to the knowledge of mankind; and if they make such additions to the knowledge of mankind, they will be preparing the materials of a new tone and of new splendors in the realm of literature. There is a sunrise and sunset. There is a transition from the light of the sun to the gentler light of the moon. There is a rest in nature which seems necessary in all her great operations. And so with all the great operations of the human mind. But do not let us despond if we seem to see a diminished efficacy in the production of what is essentially and immortally great. Our sun is hidden only for a moment. It is like the day-star of Milton:--

"Which anon repairs his drooping head, And tricks his beams, and with new spangled ore, Flames in the forehead of the morning sky."

I rejoice in an occasion like this which draws the attention of the world to topics which illustrate the union of art with literature and of literature with science, because you have a hard race to run, you have a severe competition against the attraction of external pursuits, whether those pursuits take the form of business or pleasure. It is given to you to teach lessons of the utmost importance to mankind, in maintaining the principle that no progress can be real which is not equable, which is not proportionate, which does not develop all the faculties belonging to our nature. If a great increase of wealth in a country takes place, and with that increase of wealth a powerful stimulus to the invention of mere luxury, that, if it stands alone, is not, never can be, progress. It is only that one-sided development which is but one side of deformity. I hope we shall have no one-sided development. One mode of avoiding it is to teach the doctrine of that sisterhood you have asserted to-day, and confident I am that the good wishes you have exprest on behalf of literature will be re-echoed in behalf of art wherever men of letters are found.

ADDRESS OF WELCOME[1]

BY OLIVER WENDELL HOLMES

Brothers of the Association of the Alumni:--It is your misfortune and mine that you must accept my services as your presiding officer of the day in the place of your retiring president. I shall not be believed if I say how unwillingly it is that for the second time I find myself in this trying position; called upon to fill, as I best may, the place of one whose presence and bearing, whose courtesy, whose dignity, whose scholarship, whose standing among the distinguished children of the university, fit him alike to guide your councils and to grace your festivals. The name of Winthrop has been so long associated with the State and with the college that to sit under his mild empire is like resting beneath one of these wide-branching elms the breadth of whose shade is only a measure of the hold its roots have taken in the soil. In the midst of civil strife we, the children of this our common mother, have come together in peace. And surely there never was a time when we more needed a brief respite in some chosen place of refuge, some unviolated sanctuary, from the cares and anxieties of our daily existence than at this very hour. Our life has grown haggard with excitement. The rattle of drums, the march of regiments, the gallop of squadrons, the roar of artillery, seem to have been continually sounding in our ears day and night, sleeping and waking, for two long years and more. How few of us have not trembled and shuddered with fear over and over again for those whom we love. Alas! how many that hear me have mourned over the lost--lost to earthly sight, but immortal in our love and their country's honor! We need a little breathing-space to rest from our anxious thoughts, and, as we look back to the tranquil days we passed in this still retreat, to dream of that future when in God's good time, and after his wise purpose is fulfilled, the fair angel who has so long left us shall lay her hand upon the leaping heart of this embattled nation and whisper, "Peace! be still!"

Here of all places in the world we may best hope to find the peace we seek for. It seems as if nothing were left undisturbed in New England except here and there an old graveyard, and these dear old College buildings, with the trees in which they are embowered. The old State House is filled with those that sell oxen and sheep and doves, and the changers of money. The Hancock house, the umbilical scar of the cord that held our city to the past, is vanishing like a dimple from the water.

But Massachusetts, venerable old Massachusetts, stands as firm as ever; Hollis, this very year a centenarian, is waiting with its honest red face in a glow of cordiality to welcome its hundredth set of inmates; Holden Chapel, with the skulls of its Doric frieze and the unpunishable cherub over its portals, looks serenely to the sunsets; Harvard, within whose ancient walls we are gathered, and whose morning bell has murdered sleep for so many generations of drowsy adolescents, is at its post, ready to startle the new-fledged freshmen from their first uneasy slumbers. All these venerable edifices stand as they did when we were boys,--when our grandfathers were boys. Let not the rash hand of innovation violate their sanctities, for the cement that knits these walls is no vulgar mortar, but is tempered with associations and memories which are stronger than the parts they bind together!

We meet on this auspicious morning forgetting all our lesser differences. As we enter these consecrated precincts, the livery of our special tribe in creed and in politics is taken from us at the door, and we put on the court dress of our gracious Queen's own ordering, the academic robe, such as we wore in those bygone years scattered along the seven last decades. We are not forgetful of the honors which our fellow students have won since they received their college "parts,"--their orations, dissertations, disquisitions, colloquies, and Greek dialogs. But to-day we have no rank; we are all first scholars. The hero in his laurels sits next to the divine rustling in the dry garlands of his doctorate. The poet in his crown of bays, the critic, in his wreath of ivy, clasp each other's hands, members of the same happy family. This is the birthday feast for every one of us whose forehead has been sprinkled from the font inscribed "Christo et Ecclesioe." We have no badges but our diplomas, no distinctions but our years of graduation. This is the republic carried into the university; all of us are born equal into this great fraternity.

Welcome, then, welcome, all of you, dear brothers, to this our joyous meeting! We must, we will call it joyous, tho it comes with many saddening thoughts. Our last triennial meeting was a festival in a double sense, for the same day that brought us together at our family gathering gave a new head to our ancient household of the university. As I look to-day in vain for his stately presence and kindly smile, I am reminded of the touching words spoken by an early president of the university in the remembrance of a loss not unlike our own. It was at the commencement exercises of the year 1678 that the Reverend President Urian Oakes thus mourned for his friend Thomas Shepard, the minister of Charlestown, an overseer of the college: "Dici non potest quam me perorantem, in comitiis, conspectus ejus, multo jucundissimus, recrearit et refecerit. At non comparet hodie Shepardus in his comitiis; oculos huc illuc torqueo; quocumque tamen inciderint, Platonem meum intanta virorum illustrium frequentia requirunt; nusquam amicum et pernecessarium meum in hac solenni panegyric, inter nosce Reverendos Theologos, Academiae Curatores, reperire aut oculis vestigare possum." Almost two hundred years have gone by since these words were uttered by the fourth president of the college, which I repeat as no unfitting tribute to the memory of the twentieth, the rare and fully ripened scholar who was suddenly ravished from us as some richly freighted argosy that just reaches her harbor and sinks under a cloudless sky with all her precious treasures.

But the great conflict through which we are passing has made sorrow too frequent a guest for us to linger on an occasion like this over every beloved name which the day recalls to our memory. Many of the children whom our mother had trained to arts have given the freshness of their youth or the strength of their manhood to arms. How strangely frequent in our recent record is the sign interpreted by the words "E vivis cesserunt stelligeri!" It seems as if the red war-planet had replaced the peaceful star, and these pages blushed like a rubric with the long list of the martyr-children of our university. I can not speak their eulogy, for there are no phrases in my vocabulary fit to enshrine the memory of the Christian warrior,--of him--

"Who, doomed to go in company with Pain And Fear and Bloodshed, miserable train, Turns his necessity to glorious gain--"

"Who, whether praise of him must walk the earth Forever, and to noble deeds give birth, Or he must fall, to sleep without his fame, And leave a dead, unprofitable name, Finds comfort in himself and in his cause; And while the mortal mist is gathering, draws His breath in confidence of Heaven's applause."

Yet again, O brothers! this is not the hour for sorrow. Month after month until the months became years we have cried to those who stood upon our walls: "Watchmen, what of the night?" They have answered again and again, "The dawn is breaking,--it will soon be day." But the night has gathered round us darker than before. At last--glory be to God in the highest!--at last we ask no more tidings of the watchmen, for over both horizons east and west bursts forth in one overflowing tide of radiance the ruddy light of victory!

We have no parties here to-day, but is there one breast that does not throb with joy as the banners of the conquering Republic follow her retreating foes to the banks of the angry Potomac? Is there one heart that does not thrill in answer to the drum-beat that rings all over the world as the army of the west, on the morning of the nation's birth, swarms over the silent, sullen earthworks of captured Vicksburg,--to the reveille that calls up our Northern regiments this morning inside the fatal abatis of Port Hudson? We are scholars, we are graduates, we are alumni, we are a band of brothers, but beside all, above all, we are American citizens. And now that hope dawns upon our land--nay, bursts upon it in a flood of glory,--shall we not feel its splendors reflected upon our peaceful gathering, peaceful in spite of those disturbances which the strong hand of our citizen-soldiery has already strangled?

Welcome then, thrice welcome, scholarly soldiers who have fought for your and our rights and honor! Welcome, soldierly scholars who are ready to fight whenever your country calls for your services! Welcome, ye who preach courage as well as meekness, remembering that the Prince of Peace came also bringing a sword! Welcome, ye who make and who interpret the statutes which are meant to guard our liberties in peace, but not to aid our foes in war! Welcome, ye whose healing ministry soothes the anguish of the suffering and the dying with every aid of art and the tender accents of compassion! Welcome, ye who are training the generous youths to whom our country looks as its future guardians! Welcome, ye quiet scholars who in your lonely studies are unconsciously shaping the thought which law shall forge into its shield and war shall wield as its thunder-bolt!

And to you, Mr. President, called from one place of trust and honor to rule over the concerns of this our ancient and venerated institution, to you we offer our most cordial welcome with all our hopes and prayers for your long and happy administration.

I give you, brothers, "The association of the Alumni"; the children of our common mother recognize the man of her choice as their new father, and would like to hear him address a few words to his numerous family.

FOOTNOTE:

[1] Delivered at an Alumni Dinner, Cambridge, July 16, 1863.

GOOD WILL TO AMERICA[2]

BY SIR WILLIAM HARCOURT

Gentlemen:--Small as are the pretensions which, on any account, I can have to present myself to the attention of this remarkable assemblage, I have had no hesitation in answering the call which is just been made upon me by discharging a duty which is no less gratifying to me than I know it will be agreeable to you--that of proposing that the thanks of this meeting be offered to the chairman for his presidence over us to-day. Every one who admires Mr. Garrison for the qualities on account of which we have met to do him honor on this occasion, must feel that there is a singular appropriateness in the selection of the person who has presided here to-day. No one can fail to perceive a striking similarity--I might almost say a real parallelism of greatness--in the careers of these two eminent persons. Both are men who, by the great qualities of their minds, and the uncompromising spirit of justice which has animated them, have signally advanced the cause of truth and vindicated the rights of humanity. Both have been fortunate enough in the span of their own lifetime to have seen their efforts in the promotion of great ends crowned by triumphs as great as they could have desired, and far greater than they could have hoped. There is no cause with which the name of Mr. Bright has been associated which has not sooner or later won its way to victory.

I shall not go over the ground which has been so well dealt with by those who have preceded me. But tho there have been many abler interpreters of your wishes and aspirations to-day than I can hope to be, may I be permitted to join my voice to those which have been raised up in favor of the perpetual amity of England and America. It seems to me that with nations, as well as with individuals, greatness of character depends chiefly on the degree in which they are capable of rising above thee low, narrow, paltry interests of the present, and of looking forward with hope and with faith into the distance of a great futurity. And where, I will ask, is the future of our race to be found? I may extend the question--where is to be found the future of mankind? Who that can forecast the fortunes of the ages to come will not answer--it is in that great nation which has sprung from our loins, which is flesh of our flesh and bone of our bone. The stratifications of history are full of the skeletons of ruined kingdoms and of races that are no more. Where are Assyria and Egypt, the civilization of Greece, the universal dominion of Rome? They founded empires of conquest, which have perished by the sword by which they rose. Is it to be with us as with them? I hope not--I think not. But if the day of our decline should arise, we shall at least have the consolation of knowing that we have left behind us a race which shall perpetuate our name and reproduce our greatness. Was there ever parent who had juster reason to be proud of its offspring? Was there ever child that had more cause for gratitude to its progenitor? From whom but us did America derive those institutions of liberty, those instincts of government, that capacity of greatness, which have made her what she is, and which will yet make her that which she is destined to become? These are things which it becomes us both to remember and to think upon. And, therefore, it is that, as our distinguished guest, with innate modesty, has already said, this is not a mere personal festivity--this is no occasional compliment. We see in it a deeper and wider significance. We celebrate in it the union of two nations. While I ask you to return your thanks to our chairman I think I may venture also to ask of our guest a boon which he will not refuse us. We have a great message to send, and we have here a messenger worthy to bear it. I will ask Mr. Garrison to carry back to his home the prayer of this assembly and of this nation that there may be forever and forever peace and good will between England and America. For the good will of America and England is nothing less than the evangel of liberty and of peace. And who more worthy to preside over such a gospel than the chairman to whom I ask you to return your thanks to-day? I beg to propose that the thanks of the meeting be given to Mr. Bright.

FOOTNOTE:

[2] Speech at breakfast held in London in honor of Mr. Garrison, June 29,

1867.

THE QUALITIES THAT WIN

BY CHARLES SUMNER

Mr. President and Brothers of New England:--For the first time in my life I have the good fortune to enjoy this famous anniversary festival. Tho often honored by your most tempting invitation, and longing to celebrate the day in this goodly company of which all have heard so much, I could never excuse myself from duties in another place. If now I yield to well-known attractions, and journey from Washington for my first holiday during a protracted public service, it is because all was enhanced by the appeal of your excellent president, to whom I am bound by the friendship of many years in Boston, in New York, and in a foreign land. It is much to be a brother of New England, but it is more to be a friend, and this tie I have pleasure in confessing to-night.

It is with much doubt and humility that I venture to answer for the Senate of the United States, and I believe the least I say on this head will be the most prudent. But I shall be entirely safe in expressing my doubt if there is a single Senator who would not be glad of a seat at this generous banquet. What is the Senate? It is a component part of the National Government. But we celebrate to-day more than any component part of any government. We celebrate an epoch in the history of mankind--not only never to be forgotten, but to grow in grandeur as the world appreciates the elements of true greatness. Of mankind I say--for the landing on Plymouth Rock, on December 22, 1620, marks the origin of a new order of ages, which the whole human family will be elevated. Then and there was the great beginning.

Throughout all time, from the dawn of history, men have swarmed to found new homes in distant lands. The Tyrians, skirting Northern Africa, stopt at Carthage; Carthaginians dotted Spain and even the distant coasts of Britain and Ireland; Greeks gemmed Italy and Sicily with art-loving settlements; Rome carried multitudinous colonies with her conquering eagles. Saxons, Danes, and Normans violently mingled with the original Britons. And in modern times, Venice, Genoa, Portugal, Spain, France, and England, all sent forth emigrants to people foreign shores. But in these various expeditions, trade or war was the impelling motive. Too often commerce and conquest moved hand in hand, and the colony was incarnadined with blood.

On the day we celebrate, the sun for the first time in his course looked down upon a different scene, begun and continued under a different inspiration. A few conscientious Englishmen, in obedience to the monitor within, and that they might be free to worship God according to their own sense of duty, set sail for the unknown wilds of the North American continent. After a voyage of sixty-four days in the ship Mayflower, with Liberty at the prow and Conscience at the helm, they sighted the white sandbanks of Cape Cod, and soon thereafter in the small cabin framed that brief compact, forever memorable, which is the first written constitution of government in human history, and the very corner-stone of the American Republic; and then these Pilgrims landed.

This compact was not only foremost in time, it was also august in character, and worthy of perpetual example. Never before had the object of the "civil body public" been announced as "to enact, constitute, and frame such just and equal laws, ordinances, acts, constitutions, and offices from time to time as shall be thought most meet and convenient for the general good of the colony." How lofty! how true! Undoubtedly, these were the grandest words of government with the largest promise of any at that time uttered.

If more were needed to illustrate the new epoch, it would be found in the parting words of the venerable pastor, John Robinson, addrest to the Pilgrims, as they were about to sail from Delfshaven--words often quoted, yet never enough. How sweetly and beautifully he says: "And if God should reveal anything to you by any other instrument of his, be as ready to receive it as ever you were to receive any truth by my ministry; but I am confident that the Lord hath more light and truth yet to break forth out of his holy word." And then how justly the good preacher rebukes those who close their souls to truth! "The Lutherans, for example, can not be drawn to go beyond what Luther saw, and whatever part of God's will he hath further imparted to Calvin, they will rather die than embrace, and so the Calvinists stick where he left them. This is a misery much to be lamented, for tho they were precious, shining lights in their times, God hath not revealed his whole will to them." Beyond the merited rebuke, here is a plain recognition of the law of human progress little discerned at the time, which teaches the sure advance of the human family, and opens the vista of the ever-broadening, never-ending future on earth.

Our Pilgrims were few and poor. The whole outfit of this historic voyage, including ?,700 of trading stock, was only ?,400, and how little was required for their succor appears in the experience of the soldier Captain Miles Standish, who, being sent to England for assistance--not military, but financial--(God save the mark!) succeeded in borrowing--how much do you suppose?--?50 sterling. Something in the way of help; and the historian adds, "tho at fifty per cent. interest." So much for a valiant soldier on a financial expedition. A later agent, Allerton, was able to borrow for the colony 100 at a reduced interest of thirty per cent. Plainly, the money-sharks of our day may trace an undoubted pedigree to these London merchants. But I know not if any son of New England, opprest by exorbitant interest, will be consoled by the thought that the Pilgrims paid the same.

And yet this small people--so obscure and outcast in condition--so slender in numbers and in means--so entirely unknown to the proud and great--so absolutely without name in contemporary records--whose departure from the Old World took little more than the breath of their bodies--are now illustrious beyond the lot of men; and the Mayflower is immortal beyond the Grecian Argo, or the stately ship of any victorious admiral. Tho this was little foreseen in their day, it is plain now how it has come to pass. The highest greatness surviving time and storm is that which proceeds from the soul of man. Monarchs and cabinets, generals and admirals, with the pomp of courts and the circumstance of war, in the gradual lapse of time disappear from sight; but the pioneers of truth, tho poor and lowly, especially those whose example elevates human nature and teaches the rights of man, so that government of the people, by the people, and for the people shall not perish from the earth, such harbingers can never be forgotten, and their renown spreads co-extensive with the cause they served.

I know not if any whom I now have the honor of addressing have thought to recall the great in rank and power filling the gaze of the world as the Mayflower with her company fared forth on their adventurous voyage. The foolish James was yet on the English throne, glorying that he had "peppered the Puritans." The morose Louis XIII, through whom Richelieu ruled, was King of France. The imbecile Philip III swayed Spain and the Indies. The persecuting Ferdinand the Second, tormentor of Protestants, was Emperor of Germany.

Paul V, of the House of Borghese, was Pope of Rome. In the same princely company and all contemporaries were Christian IV, King of Denmark, and his son Christian, Prince of Norway; Gustavus Adolphus, King of Sweden; Sigmund the Third, King of Poland; Frederick, King of Bohemia, with his wife, the unhappy Elizabeth of England, progenitor of the House of Hanover; George William, Margrave of Brandenburg, and ancestor of the Prussian house that has given an emperor to Germany; Maximilian, Duke of Bavaria; Maurice, landgrave of Hesse; Christian, Duke of Brunswick and Lunenburg; John Frederick, Duke of Wetemberg and Teck; John, Count of Nassau; Henry, Duke of Lorraine; Isabella, Infanta of Spain and ruler of the Low Countries; Maurice, fourth Prince of Orange; Charles Emanuel, Duke of Savoy and ancestor of the King of United Italy; Cosmo d?Medici, third Grand Duke of Florence; Antonio Priuli, ninety-third Doge of Venice, just after the terrible tragedy commemorated on the English stage as "Venice Preserved"; Bethlehem Gabor, Prince of Unitarian Transylvania, and elected King of Hungary, with the countenance of an African; and the Sultan Mustapha, of Constantinople, twentieth ruler of the Turks.

Such at that time were the crowned sovereigns of Europe, whose names were mentioned always with awe, and whose countenances are handed down by art, so that at this day they are visible to the curious as if they walked these streets. Mark now the contrast. There was no artist for our forefathers, nor are their countenances now known to men; but more than any powerful contemporaries at whose tread the earth trembled is their memory sacred. Pope, emperor, king, sultan, grand-duke, duke, doge, margrave, landgrave, count--what are they all by the side of the humble company that landed on Plymouth Rock? Theirs indeed, were the ensigns of worldly power, but our Pilgrims had in themselves that inborn virtue which was more than all else besides, and their landing was an epoch.

Who in the imposing troop of worldly grandeur is now remembered but with indifference or contempt? If I except Gustavus Adolphus, it is because he revealed a superior character. Confront the Mayflower and the Pilgrims with the potentates who occupied such space in the world. The former are ascending into the firmament, there to shine forever, while the latter have been long dropping into the darkness of oblivion, to be brought forth only to point a moral or illustrate the fame of contemporaries whom they regarded not. Do I err in supposing this an illustration of the supremacy which belongs to the triumphs of the moral nature? At first impeded or postponed, they at last prevail. Theirs is a brightness which, breaking through all clouds, will shine forth with ever-increasing splendor. I have often thought that if I were a preacher, if I had the honor to occupy the pulpit so grandly filled by my friend near me, one of my sermons should be from the text, "A little leaven shall leaven the whole lump." Nor do I know a better illustration of these words than the influence exerted by our Pilgrims. That small band, with the lesson of self-sacrifice, of just and equal laws, of the government of a majority, of unshrinking loyalty to principle, is now leavening this whole continent, and in the fulness of time will leaven the world. By their example, republican institutions have been commended, and in proportion as we imitate them will these institutions be assured.

Liberty, which we so much covet, is not a solitary plant. Always by its side is justice. But Justice is nothing but right applied to human affairs. Do not forget, I entreat you, that with the highest morality is the highest liberty. A great poet, in one of his inspired sonnets, speaking of his priceless possession, has said, "But who loves that must first be wise and good." Therefore do Pilgrims in their beautiful example teach liberty, teach republican institutions, as at an earlier day, Socrates and Plato, in their lessons of wisdom, taught liberty and helped the idea of the republic. If republican government has thus far failed in any experiment, as, perhaps, somewhere in Spanish America, it is because these lessons have been wanting. There have been no Pilgrims to teach the moral law.

Mr. President, with these thoughts, which I imperfectly express, I confess my obligations to the forefathers of New England, and offer to them the homage of a grateful heart. But not in thanksgiving only would I celebrate their memory. I would if I could make their example a universal lesson, and stamp it upon the land. The conscience which directed them should be the guide for our public councils. The just and equal laws which they required should be ordained by us, and the hospitality to truth which was their rule should be ours. Nor would I forget their courage and stedfastness. Had they turned back or wavered, I know not what would have been the record of this continent, but I see clearly that a great example would have been lost. Had Columbus yielded to his mutinous crew and returned to Spain without his great discovery; had Washington shrunk away disheartened by British power and the snows of New Jersey, these great instances would have been wanting for the encouragement of men. But our Pilgrims belong to the same heroic company, and their example is not less precious.

Only a short time after the landing on Plymouth Rock, the great republican poet, John Milton, wrote his "Comus," so wonderful for beauty and truth. His nature was more refined than that of the Pilgrims, and yet it requires little effort of imagination to catch from one of them, or at least from their beloved pastor, the exquisite, almost angelic words at the close--

"Mortals, who would follow me, Love Virtue; she alone is free; She can teach ye how to climb Higher than the sphery chime. Or if Virtue feeble were, Heaven itself would stoop to her."

THE ENGLISH-SPEAKING RACE

BY GEORGE WILLIAM CURTIS

Mr. Chairman and Gentlemen of the Chamber of Commerce:--I rise with some trepidation to respond to this toast, because we have been assured upon high authority, altho after what we have heard this evening we can not believe it, that the English-speaking race speaks altogether too much. Our eloquent Minister in England recently congratulated the Mechanics' Institute at Nottingham that it had abolished its debating club, and said that he gladly anticipated the establishment in all great institutions of education of a professorship of Silence. I confess that the proposal never seemed to me so timely and wise as at this moment. If I had only taken a high degree in silence, Mr. Chairman, how cordially you would congratulate me and this cheerful company!

When Mr. Phelps proceeded to say that Americans are not allowed to talk all the time, and that our orators are turned loose upon the public only once in four years, I was lost in admiration of the boundless sweep of his imagination. But when he said that the result of this quadrennial outburst was to make the country grateful that it did not come oftener, I saw that his case required heroic treatment, and must be turned over to Dr. Depew.

I am sure, at least, that when our distinguished friends from England return to their native land they will hasten to besiege His Excellency to tell them where the Americans are kept who speak only once in four years. And if they will but remain through the winter, they will discover that if our orators are turned loose upon the public only once in four years, they are turned loose in private all the rest of the time; and if the experience and observation of our guests are as fortunate as mine, they will learn that there are certain orators of both branches of the English-speaking race--not one hundred miles from me at this moment--whom the public would gladly hear, if they were turned loose upon it every four hours.

Wendell Phillips used to say that as soon as a Yankee baby could sit up in his cradle, he called the nursery to order and proceeded to address the house. If this Parliamentary instinct is irrepressible, if all the year round we are listening to orations, speeches, lectures, sermons, and the incessant, if not always soothing, oratory of the press, to which His Honor the Mayor is understood to be a closely attentive listener, we have at least the consolation of knowing that the talking countries are the free countries, and that the English-speaking races are the invincible legions of liberty.

The sentiment which you have read, Mr. Chairman, describes in a few comprehensive words the historic characteristics of the English-speaking race. That it is the founder of commonwealths, let the miracle of empire which we have wrought upon the Western Continent attest:--its advance from the seaboard with the rifle and the ax, the plow and the shuttle, the teapot and the Bible, the rocking-chair and the spelling-book, the bath-tub and a free constitution, sweeping across the Alleghanies, over-spreading the prairies and pushing on until the dash of the Atlantic in their ears dies in the murmur of the Pacific; and as the wonderful Goddess of the old mythology touched earth, flowers and fruits answered her footfall, so in the long trail of this advancing race, it has left clusters of happy States, teeming with a population, man by man, more intelligent and prosperous than ever before the sun shone upon, and each remoter camp of that triumphal march is but a further outpost of English-speaking civilization.

That it is the pioneer of progress, is written all over the globe to the utmost islands of the sea, and upon every page of the history of civil and religious and commercial freedom. Every factory that hums with marvelous machinery, every railway and steamer, every telegraph and telephone, the changed systems of agriculture, the endless and universal throb and heat of magical invention, are, in their larger part, but the expression of the genius of the race that with Watts drew from the airiest vapor the mightiest of motive powers, with Franklin leashed the lightning, and with Morse outfabled fairy lore. The race that extorted from kings the charter of its political rights has won, from the princes and powers of the air, the earth and the water, the secret of supreme dominion, the illimitable franchise of beneficent progress.

That it is the stubborn defender of liberty, let our own annals answer, for America sprang from the defense of English liberty in English colonies, by men of English blood, who still proudly speak the English language, cherish English traditions, and share of right, and as their own, the ancient glory of England.

No English-speaking people could, if it would, escape its distinctive name, and, since Greece and Judea, no name has the same worth and honor among men. We Americans may flout England a hundred times. We may oppose her opinions with reason, we may think her views unsound, her policy unwise; but from what country would the most American of Americans prefer to have derived the characteristic impulse of American development and civilization rather than England? What language would we rather speak than the tongue of Shakespeare and Hampden, of the Pilgrims and King James's version? What yachts, as a tribute to ourselves upon their own element, would we rather outsail than English yachts? In what national life, modes of thought, standards and estimates of character and achievement do we find our own so perfectly reflected as in the English House of Commons, in English counting-rooms and workshops, and in English homes?

No doubt the original stock has been essentially modified in the younger branch. The American, as he looks across the sea, to what Hawthorne happily called "Our old home," and contemplates himself, is disposed to murmur: "Out of the eater shall come forth meat and out of the strength shall come forth sweetness." He left England a Puritan iconoclast; he has developed in Church and State into a constitutional reformer. He came hither a knotted club; he has been transformed into a Damascus blade. He seized and tamed a continent with a hand of iron; he civilizes and controls it with a touch of velvet. No music is so sweet to his ear as the sound of the common-school bell; no principle so dear to his heart as the equal rights of all men; no vision so entrancing to his hope as those rights universally secured.

This is the Yankee; this is the younger branch; but a branch of no base or brittle fiber, but of the tough old English oak, which has weathered triumphantly the tempest of a thousand years. It is a noble contention whether the younger or the elder branch has further advanced the frontiers of liberty, but it is unquestionable that liberty, as we understand it on both sides of the sea, is an English tradition; we inherit it, we possess it, we transmit it, under forms peculiar to the English race. It is as Mr. Chamberlain has said, liberty under law. It is liberty, not license; civilization, not barbarism; it is liberty clad in the celestial robe of law, because law is the only authoritative expression of the will of the people, representative government, trial by jury, habeas corpus, freedom of speech and of the press--why, Mr. Chairman, they are the family heirlooms, the family diamonds, and they go wherever in the wide world go the family name and language and tradition.

Sir, with all my heart, and, I am sure, with the hearty assent of this great and representative company, I respond to the final aspiration of your toast: "May this great family in all its branches ever work together for the world's welfare." Certainly its division and alienation would be the world's misfortune. That England and America have had sharp and angry quarrels is undeniable. Party spirit in this country, recalling old animosity, has always stigmatized with the English name whatever it opposed. Every difference, every misunderstanding with England has been ignobly turned to party account; but the two great branches of this common race have come of age, and wherever they may encounter a serious difficulty which must be accommodated they have but to thrust demagogues aside, to recall the sublime words of Abraham Lincoln, "With malice toward none, with charity for all," and in that spirit, and in the spirit and the emotion represented in this country by the gentlemen upon my right and my left, I make bold to say to Mr. Chamberlain, in your name, there can be no misunderstanding which may not be honorably and happily adjusted. For to our race, gentlemen of both countries, is committed not only the defense, but the illustration of constitutional liberty.

The question is not what we did a century ago, or in the beginning of this century, with the lights that shone around us, but what is our duty to-day, in the light which is given to us of popular government under the republican form in this country, and the parliamentary form in England.

If a sensitive public conscience, if general intelligence should not fail to secure us from unnatural conflict, then liberty will not be justified of her children, and the glory of the English-speaking race will decline. I do not believe it. I believe that it is constantly increasing, and that the colossal power which slumbers in the arms of a kindred people will henceforth be invoked, not to drive them further asunder, but to weld them more indissolubly together in the defense of liberty under law.

WOMAN

BY HORACE PORTER

Mr. President and Gentlemen:--When this toast was proposed to me, I insisted that it ought to be responded to by a bachelor, by some one who is known as a ladies' man; but in these days of female proprietorship it is supposed that a married person is more essentially a ladies' man than anybody else, and it was thought that only one who had the courage to address a lady could have the courage, under these circumstances, to address the New England Society.

The toast, I see, is not in its usual order to-night. At public dinners this toast is habitually placed last on the list. It seems to be a benevolent provision of the Committee on Toasts in order to give man in replying to Woman one chance at least in life of having the last word. At the New England dinners, unfortunately the most fruitful subject of remark regarding woman is not so much her appearance as her disappearance. I know that this was remedied a few years ago, when this grand annual gastronomic high carnival was held in the Metropolitan Concert Hall. There, ladies were introduced into the galleries to grace the scene by their presence; and I am sure the experiment was sufficiently encouraging to warrant repetition, for it was beautiful to see the descendants of the Pilgrims sitting with eyes upturned in true Puritanic sanctity it was encouraging to see the sons of those pious sires devoting themselves, at least for one night, to setting their affections upon "things above."

Woman's first home was in the Garden of Eden. There man first married woman. Strange that the incident should have suggested to Milton the

"Paradise Lost." Man was placed in a profound sleep, a rib was taken from his side, a woman was created from it, and she became his wife. Evil-minded persons constantly tell us that thus man's first sleep became his last repose. But if woman be given at times to that contrariety of thought and perversity of mind which sometimes passeth our understanding, it must be recollected in her favor that she was created out of the crookedest part of man.

The Rabbins have a different theory regarding creation. They go back to the time when we were all monkeys. They insist that man was originally created with a kind of Darwinian tail, and that in the process of evolution this caudal appendage was removed and created into woman. This might better account for those Caudle lectures which woman is in the habit of delivering, and some color is given to this theory, from the fact that husbands even down to the present day seem to inherit a general disposition to leave their wives behind.

The first woman, finding no other man in that garden except her own husband, took to flirting even with the Devil. The race might have been saved much tribulation if Eden had been located in some calm and tranquil land-- like Ireland. There would at least have been no snakes there to get into the garden. Now woman in her thirst after knowledge, showed her true female inquisitiveness in her cross-examination of the serpent, and, in commemoration of that circumstance the serpent seems to have been curled up and used in nearly all languages as a sign of interrogation. Soon the domestic troubles of our first parents began. The first woman's favorite son was killed with a club, and married women even to this day seem to have an instinctive horror of clubs. The first woman learned that it was Cain that raised a club. The modern woman has learned that it is a club that raises cain. Yet, I think, I recognize faces here to-night that I see behind the windows of Fifth Avenue clubs of an afternoon, with their noses pressed flat against the broad plate glass, and as woman trips along the sidewalk, I have observed that these gentlemen appear to be more assiduously engaged than ever was a government scientific commission, in taking observations upon the transit of Venus.

Before those windows passes many a face fairer than that of the Ludovician Juno or the Venus of Medici. There is the Saxon blonde with the deep blue eye, whose glances return love for love, whose silken tresses rest upon her shoulders like a wealth of golden fleece, each thread of which looks like a ray of the morning sunbeam. There is the Latin brunette with the deep, black, piercing eye, whose jetty lashes rest like a silken fringe upon the pearly texture of her dainty cheek, looking like raven's wings spread out upon new-fallen snow.

And yet the club man is not happy. As the ages roll on woman has materially elevated herself in the scale of being. Now she stops at nothing. She soars. She demands the co-education of sexes. She thinks nothing of delving into the most abstruse problems of the higher branches of analytical science. She can cipher out the exact hour of the night when her husband ought to be home, either according to the old or the recently adopted method of calculating time. I never knew of but one married man who gained any decided domestic advantage by this change in our time. He was a habitu?of a club situated next door to his house. His wife was always upbraiding him for coming home too late at night. Fortunately, when they made this change of time, they placed one of those meridians from which our time is calculated right between the club and his house. Every time he stept across that imaginary line it set him back a whole hour in time. He found that he could then leave his club at one o'clock and get home to his wife at twelve; and for the first time in twenty years peace reigned around the hearthstone.

Woman now revels even in the more complicated problems of mathematical astronomy. Give a woman ten minutes and she will describe a heliocentric parallax of the heavens. Give her twenty minutes and she will find astronomically the longitude of a place by means of lunar culminations. Give that same woman an hour and a half with the present fashions, and she can not find the pocket in her dress.

And yet man's admiration for woman never flags. He will give her half his fortune; he will give her his whole heart; he seems always willing to give her everything that he possesses, except his seat in a horse-car.

Every nation has had its heroines as well as its heroes. England, in her wars, had a Florence Nightingale; and the soldiers in the expression of their adoration, used to stoop and kiss the hem of her garment as she passed. America, in her war, had a Dr. Mary Walker. Nobody ever stooped to kiss the hem of her garment--because that was not exactly the kind of a garment she wore. But why should man stand here and attempt to speak for woman, when she is so abundantly equipped to speak for herself. I know that is the case in New England; and I am reminded, by seeing General Grant here to-night, of an incident in proof of it which occurred when he was making that marvelous tour through New England, just after the war. The train stopt at a station in the State of Maine. The General was standing on the rear platform of the last car. At that time, as you know, he had a great reputation for silence--for it was before he had made his series of brilliant speeches before the New England Society. They spoke of his reticence--a quality which New Englanders admire so much--in others. Suddenly there was a commotion in the crowd, and as it opened a large, tall, gaunt-looking woman came rushing toward the car, out of breath. Taking her spectacles off from the top of her head and putting them on her nose, she put her arms akimbo, and looking up, said: "Well, I've just come down here a runnin' nigh onto two mile, right on the clean jump, just to get a look at the man that lets the women do all the talkin'."

The first regular speaker of the evening (William M. Evarts) touched upon woman, but only incidentally, only in reference to Mormonism and that sad land of Utah, where a single death may make a dozen widows.

A speaker at the New England dinner in Brooklyn last night (Henry Ward Beecher) tried to prove that the Mormons came originally from New Hampshire and Vermont. I know that a New Englander sometimes in the course of his life marries several times; but he takes the precaution to take his wives in their proper order of legal succession. The difference is that he drives his team of wives tandem, while the Mormon insists upon driving his abreast.

But even the least serious of us, Mr. President, have some serious moments in which to contemplate the true nobility of woman's character. If she were created from a rib, she was made from that part which lies nearest a man's heart.

It has been beautifully said that man was fashioned out of the dust of the earth while woman was created from God's own image. It is our pride in this land that woman's honor is her own best defense; that here female virtue is not measured by the vigilance of detective nurses; that here woman may walk throughout the length and the breadth of this land, through its highways and byways, uninsulted, unmolested, clothed in the invulnerable panoply of her own woman's virtue; that even in places where crime lurks and vice prevails in the haunts of our great cities, and in the rude mining gulches of the West, owing to the noble efforts of our women, and the influence of their example, there are raised, even there, girls who are good daughters, loyal wives, and faithful mothers. They seem to rise in those rude surroundings as grows the pond lily, which is entangled by every species of rank growth, environed by poison, miasma and corruption, and yet which rises in the beauty of its purity and lifts its fair face unblushing to the sun.

No one who has witnessed the heroism of America's daughters in the field should fail to pay a passing tribute to their worth. I do not speak alone of those trained Sisters of Charity, who in scenes of misery and woe seem Heaven's chosen messengers on earth; but I would speak also of those fair daughters who come forth from the comfortable firesides of New England and other States, little trained to scenes of suffering, little used to the rudeness of a life in camp, who gave their all, their time, their health, and even life itself as a willing sacrifice in that cause which then moved the nation's soul. As one of these, with her graceful form, was seen moving silently through the darkened aisles of an army hospital, as the motion of her passing dress wafted a breeze across the face of the wounded, they felt that their parched brows had been fanned by the wings of the angel of mercy.

Ah! Mr. President, woman is after all a mystery. It has been well said, that woman is the great conundrum of the nineteenth century; but if we can not guess her, we will never give her up.

TRIBUTE TO HERBERT SPENCER

BY WILLIAM M. EVARTS

Gentlemen:--We are here to-night, to show the feeling of Americans toward our distinguished guest. As no room and no city can hold all his friends and admirers, it was necessary that a company should be made up by some method out of the mass, and what so good a method as that of natural selection and the inclusion, within these walls, of the ladies? It is a little hard upon the rational instincts and experiences of man that we should take up the abstruse subjects of philosophy and of evolution, of all the great topics that make up Mr. Spencer's contribution to the learning and the wisdom of his time, at this end of the dinner.

The most ancient nations, even in their primitive condition, saw the folly of this, and when one wished either to be inspired with the thoughts of others or to be himself a diviner of the thoughts of others, fasting was necessary, and a people from whom I think a great many things might be learned for the good of the people of the present time, have a maxim that will commend itself to your common-sense. They say the continually stuffed body can not see secret things. Now, from my personal knowledge of the men I see at these tables, they are owners of continually stuffed bodies. I have addrest them at public dinners, on all topics and for all purposes, and whatever sympathy they may have shown with the divers occasions which brought them together, they come up to this notion of continually stuffed bodies. In primitive times they had a custom which we only under the system of differentiation practise now at this dinner. When men wished to possess themselves of the learning, the wisdom, the philosophy, the courage, the great traits of any person, they immediately proceeded to eat him up as soon as he was dead, having only this diversity in that early time that he should be either roasted or boiled according as he was fat or thin. Now out of that narrow compass, see how by the process of differentiation and of multiplication of effects we have come to a dinner of a dozen courses and wines of as many varieties; and that simple process of appropriating the virtue and the wisdom of the great man that was brought before the feast is now diversified into an analysis of all the men here under the cunning management of many speakers. No doubt, preserving as we do the identity of all these institutions it is often considered a great art, or at least a great delight, to roast our friends and put in hot water those against whom we have a grudge.

Now, Mr. Spencer, we are glad to meet you here. We are glad to see you and we are glad to have you see us. We are glad to see you, for we recognize in the breadth of your knowledge, such knowledge as is useful to your race, a greater comprehension than any living man has presented to our generation. We are glad to see you, because in our judgment you have brought to the analysis and distribution of this vast knowledge a more penetrating intelligence and a more thorough insight than any living man has brought even to the minor topics of his special knowledge. In theology, in psychology, in natural science, in the knowledge of individual man and his exposition and in the knowledge of the world in the proper sense of society, which makes up the world, the world worth knowing, the world worth speaking of, the world worth planning for, the world worth working for, we acknowledge your labors as surpassing those of any of our kind. You seem to us to carry away and maintain in the future the same measure of fame among others that we are told was given in the Middle Ages to Albertus Magnus, the most learned man of those times, whose comprehension of theology, of psychology, of natural history, of politics, of history, and of learning, comprehended more than any man since the classic time certainly; and yet it was found of him that his knowledge was rather an accumulation, and that he had added no new processes and no new wealth to the learning which he had achieved.

Now, I have said that we are glad to have you see us. You have already treated us to a very unique piece of work in this reception, and we are expecting perhaps that the world may be instructed after you are safely on the other side of the Atlantic in a more intimate and thorough manner concerning our merits and our few faults. This faculty of laying on a dissecting board an entire nation or an entire age and finding out all the arteries and veins and pulsations of their life is an extension beyond any that our own medical schools afford. You give us that knowledge of man which is practical and useful, and whatever the claims or the debates may be about your system or the system of those who agree with you, and however it may be compared with other competing systems that have preceded it, we must all agree that it is practical, that it is benevolent, that it is serious and that it is reverent; that it aims at the highest results in virtue; that it treats evil, not as eternal, but as evanescent, and that it expects to arrive at what is sought through the aid of the millennium--that condition of affairs in which there is the highest morality and the greatest happiness. And if we can come to that by these processes and these instructions, it matters little to the race whether it be called scientific morality and mathematical freedom or by another less pretentious name. You will please fill your glasses while we propose the health of our guest, Herbert Spencer.

THE EMPIRE STATE[3]

MR. CHAUNCEY M. DEPEW

Mr. President and Gentlemen:--It has been my lot from a time whence I can not remember to respond each year to this toast. When I received the invitation from the committee, its originality and ingenuity astonished and overwhelmed me. But there is one thing the committee took into consideration when they invited me to this platform. This is a Presidential year, and it becomes men not to trust themselves talking on dangerous topics. The State of New York is eminently safe. Ever since the present able and distinguished Governor has held his place I have been called upon by the New England Society to respond for him. It is probably due to that element in the New Englander that he delights in provoking controversy. The Governor is a Democrat, and I am a Republican. Whatever he believes in I detest; whatever he admires I hate. The manner in which this toast is received leads me to believe that in the New England Society his administration is unanimously approved. Governor Robinson, if I understand correctly his views, would rather that any other man should have been elected as Chief Magistrate than Mr. John Kelly. Mr. Kelly, if I interpret aright his public utterances, would prefer any other man for the Governor of New York than Lucius Robinson, and therefore, in one of the most heated controversies we have ever had, we elected a Governor by unanimous consent or assent in Alonzo B. Cornell. Horace Greeley once said to me, as we were returning from a State convention where he had been a candidate, but the delegates had failed to nominate the fittest man for the place: "I don't see why any man wants to be Governor of the State of New York, for there is no one living who can name the last ten Governors on a moment's notice." But tho there have been Governors and Governors, there is, when the gubernatorial office is mentioned, one figure that strides down the centuries before all the rest; that is the old Dutch Governor of New York, with his wooden leg--Peter Stuyvesant. There have been heroines, too, who have aroused the poetry and eloquence of all times, but none who have about them the substantial aroma of the Dutch heroine, Anneke Jans.

It is within the memory of men now living when the whole of American literature was dismissed with the sneer of the Edinburgh Review, "Who reads an American book?" But out of the American wilderness a broad avenue to the highway which has been trod by the genius of all times in its march to fame was opened by Washington Irving, and in his footsteps have followed the men who are read of all the world, and who will receive the highest tributes in all times--Longfellow, and Whittier, and Hawthorne and Prescott.

New York is not only imperial in all those material results which constitute and form the greatest commonwealth in this constellation of commonwealths, but in our political system she has become the arbiter of our national destiny. As goes New York so goes the Union, and her voice indicates that the next President will be a man with New England blood in his veins or a representative of New England ideas.

And for the gentleman who will not be elected I have a Yankee story. In the Berkshire hills there was a funeral, and as they gathered in the little parlor there came the typical New England female, who mingles curiosity with her sympathy, and as she glanced around the darkened room she said to the bereaved widow, "When did you get that new eight-day clock?" "We ain't got no new eight-day clock," was the reply. "You ain't? What's that in the corner there?" "Why no, that's not an eight-day clock, that's the deceased; we stood him on end, to make room for the mourners."

Up to within fifty years ago all roads in New England led to Boston; but within the last fifty years every byway and highway in New England leads to New York. New York has become the capital of New England, and within her limits are more Yankees than in any three New England States combined. The boy who is to-day ploughing the stony hillside in New England, who is boarding around and teaching school, and who is to be the future merchant-prince or great lawyer, or wise statesman, looks not now to Boston, but to New York, as the El Dorado of his hopes. And how generously, sons of New England, have we treated you? We have put you in the best offices; we have made you our merchant-princes. Where is the city or village in our State where you do not own the best houses, run the largest manufactories, and control the principal industries? We have several times made one of your number Governor of the State, and we have placed you in positions where you honor us while we honor you. New York's choice in the National Cabinet is the distinguished Secretary of State, whose pure Yankee blood renders him none the less a most fit and most eminent representative of the Empire State.

But while we have done our best to satisfy the Yankee, there is one thing we have never been able to do. We can meet his ambition and fill his purse, but we never can satisfy his stomach. When the President stated to-night that Plymouth Rock celebrated this anniversary on the 21st, whilst we here did so on the 22d, he did not state the true reason. It is not as he said, a dispute about dates. The pork and beans of Plymouth are insufficient for the cravings of the Yankee appetite, and they chose the 21st, in order that, by the night train, they may get to New York on the 22d, to have once a year a square meal. From 1620 down to the opening of New York to their settlement, a constantly increasing void was growing inside the Yankee diaphragm, and even now the native and imported Yankee finds the best-appointed restaurant in the world sufficient for his wants; and he has migrated to this house, that he may annually have the sensation of sufficiency in the largest hotel in the United States.

My friend, Mr. Curtis, has eloquently stated, in the beginning of his address, the Dutchman's idea of the old Puritan. He has stated, at the close of his address, the modern opinion of the old Puritan. He was an uncomfortable man to live with, but two hundred years off a grand historic figure. If any one of you, gentlemen, was compelled to leave this festive board, and go back two hundred years and live with your ancestor of that day, eat his fare, drink his drink, and listen to his talk, what a time would be there, my countrymen! Before the Puritan was fitted to accomplish the work he did, with all the great opportunities that were in him, it was necessary that he should spend two years in Leyden and learn from the Dutch the important lesson of religious toleration, and the other fundamental lesson, that a common school education lies at the foundation of all civil and religious liberty. If the Dutchman had conquered Boston, it would have been a misfortune to this land, and to the world. It would have been like Diedrich Knickerbocker wrestling with an electric battery.

But when the Yankee conquered New York, his union with the Dutch formed those sterling elements which have made the Republic what it is. Yankee ideas prevailed in this land in the grandest contest in the Senate of the United States which has ever taken place, or ever will, in the victory of Nationalism over Sectionalism by the ponderous eloquence of that great defender of the Constitution, Daniel Webster. And when failing in the forum, Sectionalism took the field, Yankee ideas conquered again in that historic meeting when Lee gave up his sword to Grant. And when, in the disturbance of credit and industry which followed, the twin heresies Expansion and Repudiation stalked abroad, Yankee ideas conquered again in the policy of our distinguished guest, the Secretary of the Treasury. So great a triumph has never been won by any financial officer of the government before, as in the funding of our national debt at four per cent., and the restoration of the national credit, giving an impulse to our prosperity and industry that can neither be stayed nor stopt.

When Henry Hudson sailed up the great harbor of New York, and saw with prophetic vision its magnificent opportunities, he could only emphasize his thought, with true Dutch significance, in one sentence--"See here!" When the Yankee came and settled in New York, he emphasized his coming with another sentence--"Sit here!"--and he sat down upon the Dutchman with such force that he squeezed him out of his cabbage-patch, and upon it he built his warehouse and his residence. He found this city laid out in a beautiful labyrinth of cow-patches, with the inhabitants and the houses all standing with their gable-ends to the street, and he turned them all to the avenue, and made New York a parallelogram of palaces; and he has multiplied to such an extent that now he fills every nook of our great State, and we recognize here to-night that, with no tariff, and free trade between New England and New York, the native specimen is an improvement upon the imported article. Gentlemen, I beg leave to say, as a native New Yorker of many generations, that by the influence, the hospitality, the liberal spirit, and the cosmopolitan influences of this great State, from the unlovable Puritan of two hundred years ago you have become the most agreeable and companionable of men.

New York to-day, the Empire State of all the great States of the Commonwealth, brings in through her grand avenue to the sea eighty per cent. of all the imports, and sends forth a majority of all the exports, of the Republic. She collects and pays four-fifths of the taxes which carry on the government of the country. In the close competition to secure the great Western commerce which is to-day feeding the world and seeking an outlet along three thousand miles of coast, she holds by her commercial prestige and enterprise more than all the ports from New Orleans to Portland combined. Let us, whether native or adopted New Yorkers, be true to the past, to the present, to the future, of this commercial and financial metropolis. Let us enlarge our terminal facilities and bring the rail and the steamship close together. Let us do away with the burdens that make New York the dearest, and make her the cheapest, port on the continent; and let us impress our commercial ideas upon the national legislature, so that the navigation laws, which have driven the merchant marine of the Republic from the seas, shall be repealed, and the breezes of every clime shall unfurl, and the waves of every sea reflect, the flag of the Republic.

FOOTNOTE:

[3] Speech of Chauncey M. Depew at the seventy-fourth anniversary banquet of the New England Society in the City of New York, December 22, 1879.

MEN OF LETTERS

BY JAMES ANTHONY FROUDE

Sir Francis Grant, Your Royal Highness, My Lords, and Gentlemen:--While I feel most keenly the honor which you confer upon me in connecting my name with the interests of literature, I am embarrassed, in responding, by the nature of my subject. What is literature, and who are men of letters? From one point of view we are the most unprofitable of mankind--engaged mostly in blowing soap-bubbles. From another point of view we are the most practical and energetic portion of the community. If literature be the art of employing words skilfully in representing facts, or thoughts, or emotions, you may see excellent specimens of it every day in the advertisements in our newspapers. Every man who uses a pen to convey his meaning to others--the man of science, the man of business, the member of a learned profession-- belongs to the community of letters. Nay, he need not use his pen at all. The speeches of great orators are among the most treasured features of any national literature. The orations of Mr. Grattan are the text-books in the schools of rhetoric in the United States. Mr. Bright, under this aspect of him, holds a foremost place among the men of letters of England.

Again, sir, every eminent man, be he what he will, be he as unbookish as he pleases, so he is only eminent enough, so he holds a conspicuous place in the eyes of his countrymen, potentially belongs to us, and if not in life, then after he is gone, will be enrolled among us. The public insist on being admitted to his history, and their curiosity will not go unsatisfied. His letters are hunted up, his journals are sifted; his sayings in conversation, the doggerel which he writes to his brothers and sisters are collected, and stereotyped in print. His fate overtakes him. He can not escape from it. We cry out, but it does not appear that men sincerely resist the liberty which is taken with them. We never hear of them instructing their executors to burn their papers. They have enjoyed so much the exhibition that has been made of their contemporaries that they consent to be sacrificed themselves.

Again, sir, when we look for those who have been most distinguished as men of letters, in the usual sense of the word, where do we find them? The famous lawyer is found in his chambers, the famous artist is found in his studio. Our foremost representatives we do not find always in their libraries; we find them, in the first place, in the service of their country. ("Hear! Hear!") Owen Meredith is Viceroy of India, and all England has applauded the judgment that selected and sent him there. The right honorable gentleman (Mr. Gladstone) who three years ago was conducting the administration of this country with such brilliant success was first generally known to his countrymen as a remarkable writer. During forty years of arduous service he never wholly deserted his original calling. He is employing an interval of temporary retirement to become the interpreter of Homer to the English race, or to break a lance with the most renowned theologians in defense of spiritual liberty.

A great author, whose life we have been all lately reading with delight, contemplates the year 3000 as a period at which his works may still be studied. If any man might be led reasonably to form such an anticipation for himself by the admiration of his contemporaries, Lord Macaulay may be acquitted of vanity. The year 3000 is far away, much will happen between now and then; all that we can say with certainty of the year 3000 is that it will be something extremely different from what any one expects. I will not predict that men will then be reading Lord Macaulay's "History of England." I will not predict that they will then be reading "Lothair." But this I will say, that if any statesman of the age of Augustus or the Antonines had left us a picture of patrician society at Rome, drawn with the same skill, and with the same delicate irony with which Mr. Disraeli has described a part of English society in "Lothair," no relic of antiquity would now be devoured with more avidity and interest. Thus, sir, we are an anomalous body, with very ill-defined limits. But, such as we are, we are heartily obliged to you for wishing us well, and I give you our most sincere thanks.

LITERATURE AND POLITICS

BY JOHN MORLEY

Mr. President, Your Royal Highness, My Lords, Ladies and Gentlemen:--I feel that I am more unworthy now than I was eight years ago to figure as the representative of literature before this brilliant gathering of all the most important intellectual and social interests of our time. I have not yet been able like the Prime Minister, to go round this exhibition and see the works of art that glorify your walls; but I am led by him to expect that I shall see the pictures of Liberal leaders, including M. Rochefort. I am not sure whether M. Rochefort will figure as a man of letters or as a Liberal leader, but I can understand that his portrait would attract the Prime Minister because M. Rochefort is a politician who was once a Liberal leader, and who has now seen occasion to lose his faith in Parliamentary government. Nor have I seen the picture of "The Flowing Tide," but I shall expect to find in that picture when I do see it a number of bathing-machines in which, not the younger generation, but the elder generation, as I understand are waiting confidently--for the arrival of the "Flowing Tide," and when it arrives, the elderly gentlemen who are incarcerated in those machines will be only too anxious for a man and a horse to come and deliver them from their imminent peril.

I thought that I detected in the last words of your speech, in proposing this toast, Mr. President, an accent of gentle reproach that any one should desert the high and pleasant ways of literature for the turmoil and the everlasting contention of public life. I do not suppose that there has ever been a time in which there was less of divorce between literature and public life than the present time. There have been in the reign of the Queen two eminent statesmen who have thrice had the distinction of being Prime Minister, and oddly enough, one of those statesman (Lord Derby) has left behind him a most spirited version of Homer, while the other eminent statesman (William E. Gladstone)--happily still among us, still examines the legends and the significance of Homer. Then when we come to a period nearer to ourselves, and look at those gentlemen who have in the last six years filled the office of Minister for Ireland, we find that no fewer than three (George Otto Trevelyan, John Morley, and Arthur Balfour) were authors of books before they engaged in the very ticklish business of the government of men. And one of these three Ministers for Ireland embarked upon his literary career--which promised ample distinction--under the editorial auspices of another of the three. We possess in one branch of the Legislature the author of the most fascinating literary biography in our language. We possess also another writer whose range of knowledge and of intellectual interest is so great that he has written the most important book upon the American Commonwealth (James Bryce).

The first canon in literature was announced one hundred years ago by an eminent Frenchman who said that in literature it is your business to have preferences but no exclusions. In politics it appears to be our business to have very stiff and unchangeable preferences, and exclusion is one of the systematic objects of our life. In literature, according to another canon, you must have a free and open mind and it has been said: "Never be the prisoner of your own opinions." In politics you are very lucky if you do not have the still harder fate--(and I think that the gentlemen on the President's right hand will assent to that as readily as the gentlemen who sit on his left) of being the prisoner of other people's opinions. Of course no one can doubt for a moment that the great achievements of literature--those permanent and vital works which we will never let die--require a devotion as unceasing, as patient, as inexhaustible, as the devotion that is required for the works that adorn your walls; and we have luckily in our age--tho it may not be a literary age--masters of prose and masters of verse. No prose more winning has ever been written than that of Cardinal Newman; no verse finer, more polished, more melodious has ever been written than that of Lord Tennyson and Mr. Swinburne.

It seems to me that one of the greatest functions of literature at this moment is not merely to produce great works, but also to protect the English language--that noble, that most glorious instrument--against those hosts of invaders which I observe have in these days sprung up. I suppose that every one here has noticed the extraordinary list of names suggested lately in order to designate motion by electricity; that list of names only revealed what many of us had been observing for a long time--namely, the appalling forces that are ready at a moment's notice to deface and deform our English tongue. These strange, fantastic, grotesque, and weird titles open up to my prophetic vision a most unwelcome prospect. I tremble to see the day approach--and I am not sure that it is not approaching--when the humorists of the headlines of American journalism shall pass current as models of conciseness, energy, and color of style.

Even in our social speech this invasion seems to be taking place in an alarming degree, and I wonder what the Pilgrim Fathers of the seventeenth century would say if they could hear their pilgrim children of the nineteenth century who come over here, on various missions, and among others, "On the make." This is only one of the thousand such-like expressions which are invading the Puritan simplicity of our tongue. I will only say that I should like, for my own part, to see in every library and in every newspaper office that admirable passage in which Milton--who knew so well how to handle both the great instrument of prose and the nobler instrument of verse--declared that next to the man who furnished courage and intrepid counsels against an enemy he placed the man who should enlist small bands of good authors to resist that barbarism which invades the minds and the speech of men in methods and habits of speaking and writing.

I thank you for having allowed me the honor of saying a word as to the happiest of all callings and the most imperishable of all arts.

GENERAL SHERMAN

BY CARL SCHURZ

Gentlemen:--The adoption by the Chamber of Commerce of these resolutions which I have the honor to second, is no mere perfunctory proceeding. We have been called here by a genuine impulse of the heart. To us General Sherman was not a great man like other great men, honored and revered at a distance. We had the proud and happy privilege of calling him one of us. Only a few months ago, at the annual meeting of this Chamber, we saw the familiar face of our honorary member on this platform by the side of our President. Only a few weeks ago he sat at our banquet table, as he had often before, in the happiest mood of conviviality, and contributed to the enjoyment of the night with his always unassuming and always charming speech. And as he moved among us without the slightest pomp of self-conscious historic dignity, only with the warm and simple geniality of his nature, it would cost us sometimes an effort of the memory to recollect that he was the renowned captain who had marshaled mighty armies victoriously on many a battlefield, and whose name stood, and will forever stand, in the very foremost rank of the saviors of this Republic, and of the great soldiers of the world's history. Indeed, no American could have forgotten this for a moment; but the affection of those who were so happy as to come near to him, would sometimes struggle to outrun their veneration and gratitude.

Death has at last conquered the hero of so many campaigns; our cities and towns and villages are decked with flags at half-mast; the muffled drum and the funeral cannon boom will resound over the land as his dead body passes to the final resting-place; and the American people stand mournfully gazing into the void left by the sudden disappearance of the last of the greatest men brought forth by our war of regeneration--and this last also finally become, save Abraham Lincoln alone, the most widely beloved. He is gone; but as we of the present generation remember it, history will tell all coming centuries the romantic story of the famous "March to the Sea"--how, in the dark days of 1864, Sherman, having worked his bloody way to Atlanta, then cast off all his lines of supply and communication, and, like a bold diver into the dark unknown, seemed to vanish with all his hosts from the eyes of the world, until his triumphant reappearance on the shores of the ocean proclaimed to the anxiously expecting millions, that now the final victory was no longer doubtful, and that the Republic would surely be saved.

Nor will history fail to record that this great general was, as a victorious soldier, a model of republican citizenship. When he had done his illustrious deeds, he rose step by step to the highest rank in the army, and then, grown old, he retired. The Republic made provision for him in modest republican style. He was satisfied. He asked for no higher reward. Altho the splendor of his achievements, and the personal affection for him, which every one of his soldiers carried home, made him the most popular American of his day, and altho the most glittering prizes were not seldom held up before his eyes, he remained untroubled by ulterior ambition. No thought that the Republic owed him more ever darkened his mind. No man could have spoken to him of the "ingratitude of Republics," without meeting from him a stern rebuke. And so, content with the consciousness of a great duty nobly done, he was happy in the love of his fellow citizens.

Indeed, he may truly be said to have been in his old age, not only the most beloved, but also the happiest of Americans. Many years he lived in the midst of posterity. His task was finished, and this he wisely understood. His deeds had been passed upon by the judgment of history, and irrevocably registered among the glories of his country and his age. His generous heart envied no one, and wished every one well; and ill-will had long ceased to pursue him. Beyond cavil his fame was secure, and he enjoyed it as that which he had honestly earned, with a genuine and ever fresh delight, openly avowed by the charming frankness of his nature. He dearly loved to be esteemed and cherished by his fellow men, and what he valued most, his waning years brought him in ever increasing abundance. Thus he was in truth a most happy man, and his days went down like an evening sun in a cloudless autumn sky. And when now the American people, with that peculiar tenderness of affection which they have long borne him, lay him in his grave, the happy ending of his great life may soothe the pang of bereavement they feel in their hearts at the loss of the old hero who was so dear to them, and of whom they were and always will be so proud. His memory will ever be bright to us all; his truest monument will be the greatness of the Republic he served so well; and his fame will never cease to be prized by a grateful country, as one of its most precious possessions.

ORATION OVER ALEXANDER HAMILTON[4]

BY GOUVERNEUR MORRIS

My Friends:--If on this sad, this solemn occasion, I should endeavor to move your commiseration, it would be doing injustice to that sensibility which has been so generally and so justly manifested. Far from attempting to excite your emotions, I must try to repress my own; and yet, I fear, that instead of the language of a public speaker, you will hear only the lamentations of a wailing friend. But I will struggle with my bursting heart, to portray that heroic spirit, which has flown to the mansions of bliss.

Students of Columbia--he was in the ardent pursuit of knowledge in your academic shades when the first sound of the American war called him to the field. A young and unprotected volunteer, such was his zeal, and so brilliant his service, that we heard his name before we knew his person. It seemed as if God had called him suddenly into existence, that he might assist to save a world! The penetrating eye of Washington soon perceived the manly spirit which animated his youthful bosom. By that excellent judge of men he was selected as an aid, and thus he became early acquainted with, and was a principal actor in the more important scenes of our revolution. At the siege of

York he pertinaciously insisted on, and he obtained the command of a Forlorn Hope. He stormed the redoubt; but let it be recorded that not one single man of the enemy perished. His gallant troops, emulating the heroism of their chief checked the uplifted arm, and spared a foe no longer resisting. Here closed his military career.

Shortly after the war, your favor--no, your discernment, called him to public office. You sent him to the convention at Philadelphia; he there assisted in forming the constitution which is now the bond of our union, the shield of our defense, and the source of our prosperity. In signing the compact, he exprest his apprehension that it did not contain sufficient means of strength for its own preservation; and that in consequence we should share the fate of many other republics, and pass through anarchy to despotism. We hoped better things. We confided in the good sense of the American people; and, above all, we trusted in the protecting providence of the Almighty. On this important subject he never concealed his opinion. He disdained concealment. Knowing the purity of his heart, he bore it as it were in his hand, exposing to every passenger its inmost recesses. This generous indiscretion subjected him to censure from misrepresentation. His speculative opinions were treated as deliberate designs; and yet you all know how strenuous, how unremitting were his efforts to establish and to preserve the constitution. If, then, his opinion was wrong, pardon, O pardon, that single error, in a life devoted to your service.

At the time when our Government was organized, we were without funds, tho not without resources. To call them into action, and establish order in the finances, Washington sought for splendid talents, for extensive information, and above all, he sought for sterling, incorruptible integrity. All these he found in Hamilton. The system then adopted, has been the subject of much animadversion. If it be not without a fault, let it be remembered that nothing human is perfect. Recollect the circumstances of the moment--recollect the conflict of opinion--and, above all, remember that a minister of a republic must bend to the will of the people. The administration which Washington formed was one of the most efficient, one of the best that any country was ever blessed with. And the result was a rapid advance in power and prosperity of which there is no example in any other age or nation. The part which Hamilton bore is universally known.

His unsuspecting confidence in professions, which he believed to be sincere, led him to trust too much to the undeserving. This exposed him to misrepresentation. He felt himself obliged to resign. The care of a rising family, and the narrowness of his fortune, made it a duty to return to his profession for their support. But tho he was compelled to abandon public life, never, no, never for a moment did he abandon the public service. He never lost sight of your interests. I declare to you, before that God in whose presence we are now especially assembled, that in his most private and confidential conversations, the single objects of discussion and consideration were your freedom and happiness. You well remember the state of things which again called forth Washington from his retreat to lead your armies. You know that he asked for Hamilton to be his second in command. That venerable sage knew well the dangerous incidents of a military profession, and he felt the hand of time pinching life at its source. It was probable that he would soon be removed from the scene, and that his second would succeed to the command. He knew by experience the importance of that place--and he thought the sword of America might safely be confided to the hand which now lies cold in that coffin. Oh! my fellow citizens, remember this solemn testimonial that he was not ambitious. Yet he was charged with ambition, and, wounded by the imputation, when he laid down his command he declared in the proud independence of his soul, that he never would accept any office, unless in a foreign war he should be called on to expose his life in defense of his country. This determination was immovable. It was his fault that his opinions and his resolutions could not be changed. Knowing his own firm purpose, he was indignant at the charge that he sought for place or power. He was ambitious only for glory, but he was deeply solicitous for you. For himself he feared nothing; but he feared that bad men might, by false professions, acquire your confidence, and abuse it to your ruin.

Brethren of the Cincinnati--there lies our chief! Let him still be our model. Like him, after long and faithful public services, let us cheerfully perform the social duties of private life. Oh! he was mild and gentle. In him there was no offense; no guile. His generous hand and heart were open to all.

Gentlemen of the bar--you have lost your brightest ornament. Cherish and imitate his example. While, like him, with justifiable and laudable zeal, you pursue the interests of your clients, remember, like him, the eternal principle of justice.

Fellow citizens--you have long witnessed his professional conduct, and felt his unrivaled eloquence. You know how well he performed the duties of a citizen--you know that he never courted your favor by adulation or the sacrifice of his own judgment. You have seen him contending against you, and saving your dearest interests, as it were, in spite of yourselves. And you now feel and enjoy the benefits resulting from the firm energy of his conduct. Bear this testimony to the memory of my departed friend. I charge you to protect his fame. It is all he has left--all that these poor orphan children will inherit from their father. But, my countrymen, that fame may be a rich treasure to you also. Let it be the test by which to examine those who solicit your favor. Disregarding professions, view their conduct, and on a doubtful occasion ask, "Would Hamilton have done this thing?"

You all know how he perished. On this last scene I can not, I must not dwell. It might excite emotions too strong for your better judgment. Suffer not your indignation to lead to any act which might again offend the insulted majesty of the laws. On his part, as from his lips, tho with my voice--for his voice you will hear no more--let me entreat you to respect yourselves.

And now, ye ministers of the everlasting God, perform your holy office, and commit these ashes of our departed brother to the bosom of the grave.

FOOTNOTE:

[4] Funeral oration by Gouverneur Morris, statesman and man of affairs, pronounced before the porch of Trinity Church, New York City, over the body of Alexander Hamilton, just prior to the interment, July 14, 1804.

EULOGY OF McKINLEY

BY GROVER CLEVELAND

To-day the grave closes over the dead body of the man but lately chosen by the people of the United States from among their number to represent their nationality, preserve, protect and defend their Constitution, to faithfully execute the laws ordained for their welfare, and safely to hold and keep the honor and integrity of the Republic. His time of service is ended, not by the expiration of time, but by the tragedy of assassination. He has passed from public sight, not joyously bearing the garlands and wreaths of his countrymen's approving acclaim, but amid the sobs and tears of a mourning nation. He has gone to his home, not the habitation of earthly peace and quiet, bright with domestic comfort and joy, but to the dark and narrow house appointed for all the sons of men, there to rest until the morning light of the resurrection shall gleam in the East.

All our people loved their dead president. His kindly nature and lovable traits of character and his amiable consideration for all about him will long be in the minds and hearts of his countrymen. He loved them in return with such patriotism and unselfishness that in the hour of their grief and humiliation he would say to them: "It is God's will; I am content. If there is a lesson in my life or death, let it be taught to those who still live and have the destiny of their country in their keeping."

Let us, then, as our dead is buried out of our sight, seek for the lessons and the admonitions that may be suggested by the life and death which constitute our theme.

First in my thoughts are the lessons to be learned from the career of William McKinley by the young men who make up the student body of our university. These lessons are not obscure or difficult. They teach the value of study and mental training, but they teach more impressively that the road to usefulness and to the only success worth having, will be missed or lost except it is sought and kept by the light of those qualities of heart, which it is sometimes supposed may safely be neglected or subordinated in university surroundings. This is a great mistake. Study and study hard, but never let the thought enter your mind that study alone or the greatest possible accumulation of learning alone will lead you to the heights of usefulness and success.

The man who is universally mourned to-day achieved the highest distinction which his great country can confer on any man, and he lived a useful life. He was not deficient in education, but with all you will hear of his grand career, and of his services to his country and his fellow citizens, you will not hear that either the high place he reached or what he accomplished was due entirely to his education. You will instead constantly hear as accounting for his great success that he was obedient and affectionate as a son, patriotic and faithful as a soldier, honest and upright as a citizen, tender and devoted as a husband, and truthful, generous, unselfish, moral and clean in every relation of life. He never thought any of these things too weak for manliness. Make no mistake. Here was a most distinguished man, a great man, a useful man--who became distinguished, great and useful, because he had, and retained unimpaired, the qualities of heart which I fear university students sometimes feel like keeping in the background or abandoning.

There is a most serious lesson for all of us in the tragedy of our late president's death. The shock of it is so great that it is hard at this time to read this lesson calmly. We can hardly fail to see, however, behind the bloody deed of the assassin, horrible figures and faces from which it will not do to turn away. If we are to escape further attack upon our peace and security, we must boldly and resolutely grapple with the monster of anarchy. It is not a thing that we can safely leave to be dealt with by party or partizanship. Nothing can guarantee us against its menace except the teaching and the practise of the best citizenship, the exposure of the ends and aims of the gospel of discontent and hatred of social order, and the brave enactment and execution of repressive laws.

Our universities and colleges can not refuse to join in the battle against the tendencies of anarchy. Their help in discovering and warning against the relationship between the vicious councils and deeds of blood, and their unsteadying influence upon the elements of unrest, can not fail to be of inestimable value.

By the memory of our murdered president, let us resolve to cultivate and preserve the qualities that made him great and useful; and let us determine to meet the call of patriotic duty in every time of our country's danger or need.

DECORATION DAY[5]

BY THOMAS W. HIGGINSON

Friends:--We meet to-day for a purpose that has the dignity and the tenderness of funeral rites without their sadness. It is not a new bereavement, but one which has softened, that brings us here. We meet not around a newly opened grave, but among those which Nature has already decorated with the memorials of her love. Above every tomb her daily sunshine has smiled, her tears have wept; over the humblest she has bidden some grasses nestle, some vines creep, and the butterfly,--ancient emblem of immortality-- waves his little wings above every sod. To Nature's signs of tenderness we add our own. Not "ashes to ashes, dust to dust," but blossoms to blossoms, laurels to the laureled.

The great Civil War has passed by--its great armies were disbanded, their tents struck, their camp-fires put out, their muster-rolls laid away. But there is another army whose numbers no Presidential proclamation could reduce, no general orders disband. This is their camping-ground--these white stones are their tents--this list of names we bear is their muster-roll--their camp-fires yet burn in our hearts.

I remember this "Sweet Auburn" when no sacred associations made it sweeter, and when its trees looked down on no funerals but those of the bird and the bee. Time has enriched its memories since those days. And especially during our great war, as the Nation seemed to grow impoverished in men, these hills grow richer in associations, until their multiplying wealth took in that heroic boy who fell in almost the last battle of the war. Now that roll of honor has closed, and the work of commemoration begun.

Without distinction of nationality, of race, of religion, they gave their lives to their country. Without distinction of religion, of race, of nationality, we garland their graves to-day. The young Roman Catholic convert who died exclaiming "Mary! pardon!" and the young Protestant theological student, whose favorite place of study was this cemetery, and who asked only that no words of praise might be engraven on his stone--these bore alike the cross in their lifetime, and shall bear it alike in flowers to-day. They gave their lives that we might remain one Nation, and the Nation holds their memory alike in its arms.

And so the little distinctions of rank that separated us in the service are nothing here. Death has given the same brevet to all. The brilliant young cavalry general who rode into his last action, with stars on his shoulders and his death-wound on his breast, is to us no more precious than that sergeant of sharpshooters who followed the line unarmed at Antietam, waiting to take the rifle of some one who should die, because his own had been stolen; or that private who did the same thing in the same battle, leaving the hospital service to which he had been assigned. Nature has been equally tender to the graves of all, and our love knows no distinction.

What a wonderful embalmer is death! We who survive grow daily older. Since the war closed the youngest has gained some new wrinkle, the oldest some added gray hair. A few years more and only a few tattering figures shall represent the marching files of the Grand Army; a year or two beyond that, and there shall flutter by the window the last empty sleeve. But these who are here are embalmed forever in our imaginations; they will not change; they never will seem to us less young, less fresh, less daring, than when they sallied to their last battle. They will always have the dew of their youth; it is we alone who shall grow old.

And, again, what a wonderful purifier is death! These who fell beside us varied in character; like other men, they had their strength and their weaknesses, their merits and their faults. Yet now all stains seem washed away; their life ceased at its climax, and the ending sanctioned all that went before. They died for their country; that is their record. They found their way to heaven equally short, it seems to us, from every battle-field, and with equal readiness our love seeks them to-day.

"What is a victory like?" said a lady to the Duke of Wellington. "The greatest tragedy in the world, madam, except a defeat." Even our great war would be but a tragedy were it not for the warm feeling of brotherhood it has left behind it, based on the hidden emotions of days like these. The war has given peace to the nation; it has given union, freedom, equal rights; and in addition to that, it has given to you and me the sacred sympathy of these graves. No matter what it has cost us individually--health or worldly fortunes--it is our reward that we can stand to-day among these graves and yet not blush that we survive.

The great French soldier, de Latour d'Auvergne, was the hero of many battles, but remained by his own choice in the ranks. Napoleon gave him a sword and the official title "The First Grenadier of France." When he was killed, the Emperor ordered that his heart should be intrusted to the keeping of his regiment--that his name should be called at every roll-call, and that his next comrade should make answer, "Dead upon the field of honor." In our memories are the names of many heroes; we treasure all their hearts in this consecrated ground, and when the name of each is called, we answer in flowers, "Dead upon the field of honor."

FOOTNOTE:

[5] Delivered at Mount Auburn Cemetery, Cambridge, Mass., Decoration Day, May 30, 1870.

FAITH IN MANKIND[6]

BY ARTHUR T. HADLEY

In order to accomplish anything great, a man must have two sides to his greatness: a personal side and a social side. He must be upright himself, and he must believe in the good intentions and possibilities of others about him.

The scholars and scientific men of the country have sometimes been reproached with a certain indifference to the feelings and sentiments of their fellow men. It has been said that their critical faculty is developed more strongly than their constructive instinct; that their brain has been nourished at the expense of their heart; that what they have gained in breadth of vision has been outweighed by a loss of human sympathy.

It is for you to prove the falseness of this charge. It is for you to show by your life and utterances that you believe in the men who are working with you and about you. There will probably be times when this is a hard task. If you have studied history or literature or science aright, some things which look large to other people will look small to you. You will frequently be called upon to give the unwelcome advice that a desired end can not be reached by a short cut; and this may cause some of your enthusiastic friends to lose confidence in your leadership. There are always times when a man who is clear-headed is reproached with being hard-hearted. But if you yourselves keep your faith in your fellow men, these things, tho they be momentary hindrances, will in the long run make for your power of Christian leadership.

There was a time, not so very long ago, when the people distrusted the guidance of scientific men in things material. They believed that they could do their business best without advice of the theorists. When it came to the conduct of business, scientific men and practical men eyed each other with mutual distrust. As long as the scientific men remained mere critics this distrust remained. When they came to take up the practical problems of applied mechanics and physics and solve them positively in a large way, they became the trusted leaders of modern material development.

It is for you to deal with the profounder problems of human life in the same way. It is for you to prove your right to take the lead in the political and social and spiritual development of the country, as well as in its mechanical and material development. To do this you must take hold of these social problems with the same positive faith with which your fathers took hold of the problems of applied science. To the man who believes in his fellow men, who has faith in his country, and in whom the love of God whom he hath not seen is but an outgrowth of a love for his fellow men whom he hath seen, the opening years of the twentieth century are years of unrivaled promise. We already know that a man can learn to love God by loving his fellow men. Equally true we shall find it that a man learns to believe in God by believing in his fellow men.

FOOTNOTE:

[6] The concluding part of a baccalaureate address to the graduating class of Yale University, June 27, 1909.

WASHINGTON AND LINCOLN[7]

BY MARTIN W. LITTLETON

The strongest thing about the character of the two greatest men in American history is the fact that they did not surrender to the passion of the time. Washington withstood the French radicalism of Jefferson and the British conservatism of Hamilton. He invited each of them into his cabinet; he refused to allow either of them to dictate his policy. His enemies could not terrify him by assault; his friends could not deceive him with flattery. In this respect he resembled in marked degree the splendid character of Lincoln.

The single light that led Lincoln's feet along the hard highway of life was justice; the single thought that throbbed his brain to sleep at night was justice; the single prayer that put in whispered words the might and meaning of his soul was justice; the single impulse that lingered in a heart already wrung by a nation's grief was justice; in every word that fell from him in touching speech there was the sad and sober spirit of justice. He sat upon the storm when the nation shook with passion. Treason, wrong, injustice, crime, graft, a thousand wrongs in system and in single added to the burden of this melancholy spirit. Silently, as the soul of the just makes war on sin; silently, as the spirit of the mighty withstands the spite of wrong; silently, as the heart of the truly brave resists the assault of the coward, this prince of patience and peace endured the calumny of the country he died to save.

Lincoln blazed the way from the cabin to the crown; working away in the silence of the woods, he heard the murmur of a storm; toiling in the forest of flashing leaf and armored oak, he heard Lexington calling unto Sumter, Valley Forge crying unto Gettysburg, and Yorktown shouting unto Appomattox. Lingering before the dying fires in a humble hut, he saw with sorrowful heart the blazing camps of Virginia, and felt the awful stillness of slumbering armies. Beneath it all he saw the strained muscles of the slave, the broken spirit of the serf, the bondage of immortal souls; and beyond it all, looking through the tears that broke from a breaking heart, he saw the widow by the empty chair, the aged father's fruitless vigil at the gate, the daughter's dreary watch beside the door, and the son's solemn step from boyhood to old age. And behind this picture he saw the lonely family altar upon which was offered the incense of tears coming from millions of broken hearts; and looking still beyond he saw the battle-fields where silent slabs told of the death of those who died in deathless valor. He saw the desolated earth, where golden grain no more broke from the rich, resourceful soil, where the bannered wheat no longer rose from the productive earth; he saw the South with its smoking chimneys, its deserted hearthstones, its maimed and wounded trudging with bowed heads and bent forms back to their homes, there to want and to waste and to struggle and to build up again; he saw the North recover itself from the awful shock of arms and start anew to unite the arteries of commerce that had been cut by the cruel sword of war. And with this gentle hand, and as a last act of his sacrificial life, he dashed the awful cup of brother's blood from the lustful lip of war and shattered the cannons' roar into nameless notes of song.

Then turn to the vision of Washington leaving a plantation of peace and plenty to suffer on the blood-stained battle-field, surrendering the dominion over the princely domain of a Virginia gentleman to accept the privations of an unequal war--the vision of patriotism over against the vision of greed.

Oh, my friends, we must live so that the spirit of these men shall settle all about our lives and deeds; so that the patriotism of their service shall burn as a fire in the hearts of all who shall follow them. The Constitution which came from one, the universal liberty which came from the other, must be set in our hearts as institutions in the blood of our race, so that this Government shall not perish until every drop of that blood has been shed in its defense; and we shall behold the flag of our country as the beautiful emblem of their unselfish lives, whose red ran out of a soldier's heart, whose white was bleached by a nation's tears, whose stars were hung there to sing together until the eternal morning when all the world shall be free.

FOOTNOTE:

[7] Extract from an address on the occasion of the celebration of Washington's Birthday by the Ellicott Club of Buffalo, New York, February 22, 1906.

CHARACTERISTICS OF WASHINGTON[8]

BY WILLIAM McKINLEY

Fellow Citizens:--There is a peculiar and tender sentiment connected with this memorial. It expresses not only the gratitude and reverence of the living, but is a testimonial of affection and homage from the dead.

The comrades of Washington projected this monument. Their love inspired it. Their contributions helped to build it. Past and present share in its completion, and future generations will profit by its lessons. To participate in the dedication of such a monument is a rare and precious privilege. Every monument to Washington is a tribute to patriotism. Every shaft and statue to his memory helps to inculcate love of country, encourage loyalty and establish a better citizenship. God bless every undertaking which revives patriotism and rebukes the indifferent and lawless! A critical study of Washington's career only enhances our estimation of his vast and varied abilities.

As Commander-in-chief of the Colonial armies from the beginning of the war to the proclamation of peace, as president of the convention which framed the Constitution of the United States, and as the first President of the United States under that Constitution, Washington has a distinction differing from that of all other illustrious Americans. No other name bears or can bear such a relation to the Government. Not only by his military genius--his patience, his sagacity, his courage, and his skill--was our national independence won, but he helped in largest measure to draft the chart by which the Nation was guided; and he was the first chosen by the people to put in motion the new Government. His was not the boldness of martial display or the charm of captivating oratory, but his calm and steady judgment won men's support and commanded their confidence by appealing to their best and noblest aspirations. And withal Washington was ever so modest that at no time in his career did his personality seem in the least intrusive. He was above the temptation of power. He spurned any suggested crown. He would have no honor which the people did not bestow.

An interesting fact--and one which I love to recall--is that the only time Washington formally addrest the Constitutional Convention during all its sessions over which he presided in this city, he appealed for a larger representation of the people in the National House of Representatives, and his appeal was instantly heeded. Thus was he ever keenly watchful of the rights of the people in whose hands was the destiny of our Government then as now.

Masterful as were his military campaigns, his civil administration commands equal admiration. His foresight was marvelous; his conception of the philosophy of government, his insistence upon the necessity of education, morality, and enlightened citizenship to the progress and permanence of the Republic, can not be contemplated even at this period without filling us with astonishment at the breadth of his comprehension and the sweep of his vision. His was no narrow view of government. The immediate present was not his sole concern, but our future good his constant theme of study. He blazed the path of liberty. He laid the foundation upon which we have grown from weak and scattered Colonial governments to a united Republic whose domains and power as well as whose liberty and freedom have become the admiration of the world. Distance and time have not detracted from the fame and force of his achievements or diminished the grandeur of his life and work. Great deeds do not stop in their growth, and those of Washington will expand in influence in all the centuries to follow.

The bequest Washington has made to civilization is rich beyond computation. The obligations under which he has placed mankind are sacred and commanding. The responsibility he has left for the American people to preserve and perfect what he accomplished is exacting and solemn. Let us rejoice in every new evidence that the people realize what they enjoy and cherish with affection the illustrious heroes of Revolutionary story whose valor and sacrifices made us a nation. They live in us, and their memory will help us keep the covenant entered into for the maintenance of the freest Government of the earth.

The Nation and the name of Washington are inseparable. One is linked indissolubly with the other. Both are glorious, both triumphant. Washington lives and will live because what he did was for the exaltation of man, the enthronement of conscience, and the establishment of a Government which recognizes all the governed. And so, too, will the Nation live victorious over all obstacles, adhering to the immortal principles which Washington taught and Lincoln sustained.

FOOTNOTE:

[8] Address by William McKinley, twenty-fourth President of the United States, delivered at the unveiling of the Washington Statue, by the Society of Cincinnati, in Philadelphia, May 15, 1897.

"LET FRANCE BE FREE!"[9]

BY GEORGE JACQUES DANTON

The general considerations that have been presented to you are true; but at this moment it is less necessary to examine the causes of the disasters that have struck us than to apply their remedy rapidly. When the edifice is on fire,

I do not join the rascals who would steal the furniture, I extinguish the flames. I tell you therefore you should be convinced by the despatches of Dumouriez that you have not a moment to spare in saving the Republic.

Dumouriez conceived a plan which did honor to his genius. I would render him greater justice and praise than I did recently. But three months ago he announced to the executive power, your General Committee of Defense, that if we were not audacious enough to invade Holland in the middle of winter, to declare instantly against England the war which actually we had long been making, that we would double the difficulties of our campaign, in giving our enemies the time to deploy their forces. Since we failed to recognize this stroke of his genius we must now repair our faults.

Dumouriez is not discouraged; he is in the middle of Holland, where he will find munitions of war; to overthrow all our enemies, he wants but Frenchmen, and France is filled with citizens. Would we be free? If we no longer desire it, let us perish, for we have all sworn it. If we wish it, let all march to defend our independence. Your enemies are making their last efforts. Pitt, recognizing he has all to lose, dares spare nothing. Take Holland, and Carthage is destroyed and England can no longer exist but for Liberty! Let Holland be conquered to Liberty; and even the commercial aristocracy itself, which at the moment dominates the English people, would rise against the government which had dragged it into this despotic war against a free people. They would overthrow this ministry of stupidity who thought the methods of the ancien r 閏 ime could smother the genius of Liberty breathing in France. This ministry once overthrown in the interests of commerce the party of Liberty would show itself; for it is not dead! And if you know your duties, if your commissioners leave at once, if you extend the hand to the strangers aspiring to destroy all forms of tyranny, France is saved and the world is free.

Expedite, then, your commissioners; sustain them with your energy; let them leave this very night, this very evening.

Let them say to the opulent classes, the aristocracy of Europe must succumb to our efforts, and pay our debt, or you will have to pay it! The people have nothing but blood--they lavish it! Go, then, ingrates, and lavish your wealth! See, citizens, the fair destinies that await you. What! you have a whole nation as a lever, its reason as your fulcrum, and you have not yet upturned the world! To do this we need firmness and character, and of a truth we lack it. I put to one side all passions. They are all strangers to me save a passion for the public good.

In the most difficult situations, when the enemy was at the gates of Paris, I said to those governing: "Your discussions are shameful, I can see but the enemy. You tire me by squabbling in place of occupying yourselves with the safety of the Republic! I repudiate you all as traitors to our country! I place you all in the same line!" I said to them: "What care I for my reputation! Let France be free, tho my name were accurst! What care I that I am called 'a blood-drinker!'" Well, let us drink the blood of the enemies of humanity, if needful; but let us struggle, let us achieve freedom. Some fear the departure of the commissioners may weaken one or the other section of this Convention. Vain fears! Carry your energy everywhere. The pleasantest declaration will be to announce to the people that the terrible debt weighing upon them will be wrested from their enemies or that the rich will shortly have to pay it. The national situation is cruel. The representatives of value are no longer in equilibrium in the circulation. The day of the workingman is lengthened beyond necessity. A great corrective measure is necessary! Conquerors of Holland reanimate in England the Republican party; let us advance, France, and we shall go glorified to posterity. Achieve these grand destinies; no more debates, no more quarrels, and the fatherland is saved.

FOOTNOTE:

[9] On the disasters on the frontier--delivered in convention, March 10, 1793.

SONS OF HARVARD[10]

BY CHARLES DEVENS

The sons of Harvard who have served their country on field and flood, in deep thankfulness to Almighty God, who has covered their heads in the day of battle and permitted them to stand again in these ancient halls and under these leafy groves, sacred to so many memories of youth and learning, and in yet deeper thankfulness for the crowning mercy which has been vouchsafed in the complete triumph of our arms over rebellion, return home to-day. Educated only in the arts of peace, unlearned in all that pertained especially to the science of war, the emergency of the hour threw upon them the necessity of grasping the sword.

Claiming only that they have striven to do their duty they come only to ask their share in the common joy and happiness which our victory has diffused and meet this imposing reception. When they remember in whose presence they stand; that of all the great crowd of the sons of Harvard who are here to-day there is not one who has not contributed his utmost to the glorious consummation; that those who have been blessed with opulence have expended with the largest and most lavish hand in supplying the government with the sinews of war and sustaining everywhere the distrest upon whom the woes of war fell; that those less large in means altho not in heart have not failed to pour out most tenderly of time and care, of affection and love, in the thousand channels that have been opened; that the statesmen and legislators whose wise counsels and determined spirit have brought us thus far in safety and honor are here,--would that their task were as completely done as ours!--yet sure I am that in their hands "the pen will not lose by writing what the sword has won by fighting;" that the poets whose fiery lyrics roused us as when

"Tyrts called aloud to arms,"

and who have animated the living and celebrated the dead in the noblest strains are here; that our orators whose burning words have so cheered the gloom of the long controversy are here, altho withal we lament that one voice so often heard through the long night of gloom was not permitted to greet with us the morning. Surrounded by memories such as his, surrounded by men such as these, we may well feel at receiving this noble testimonial of your regard that it is rather you who are generous in bestowing than we who are rich in deserving. Nor do we forget the guests who honor us by their presence to-day, chief among whom we recognize his Excellency the Governor of Massachusetts, who altho he wears the civilian's coat bears as stout a heart as beats under any soldier's jacket, and who has sent his men by the thousands and tens of thousands to fight in this great battle; and the late commanding general of the Army of the Potomac under whom so many of us have fought. If the whole and comprehensive plans of our great lieutenant-general have marked him as the Ulysses of a holier and mightier epic than Homer ever dreamed, in the presence of the great captain who fairly turned the tide of the rebellion on the hills above Gettysburg, we shall not have to look far for its Achilles.

Yet, sir, speaking always of others as you have called on me to speak for them, it seems to me that the record of the sons of the university who have served in the war is not unworthy of her. In any capacity where service was honorable or useful they have rendered it. In the departments of science they have been conspicuous and the skill of the engineer upon whom we so often depended was not seldom derived from the schools of this university. In surgery they have by learning and judgment alleviated the woes of thousands. And in the ministration of that religion in whose name this university was founded they have not been less devoted; not only have cheering words gone forth from their pulpits, but they have sought the hospitals where the wounded were dying, or like Fuller at Fredericksburg, have laid down their lives on the field where armed hosts were contending. All these were applying the principles of their former education to new sets of circumstances; but, as you will remember, by far the larger portion of our number were of the combatants of the army, and the facility they displayed in adopting the profession of arms affords an admirable addition to the argument by which it has been heretofore maintained that the general education of our college was best for all who could obtain it, as affording a basis upon which any superstructure of usefulness might be raised. Readily mastering the tactics and detail of the profession, proving themselves able to grapple with its highest problems, their courage and gallantry were proverbial.

It would be a great mistake to suppose that all that was added to our army by such men as these was merely what it gained in physical force and manly prowess. Our neighbors on the other side of the water, whose attachment to monarchy is so strong that it sometimes makes them unjust to republics, have sometimes attacked the character and discipline of our army. Nothing could be more unjust. The federal army was noble, self-sacrificing, devoted always, and to the discipline of that army no men contributed more than the members of this university and men such as they. They bore always with them the loftiest principle in the contest and the highest honor in all their personal relations. Disorder in camp, pillage and plunder, found in them stern and unrelenting foes. They fought in a cause too sacred, they wore a robe too white, to be willing to stain or sully it with such corruption.

Mr. President I should ill do the duty you have called on me to perform if I forgot that this ceremonial is not only a reception of those who return, but a commemoration of those who have laid down their lives for the service of the country. He who should have properly spoken for us, the oldest of our graduates, altho not of our members who have fought in this war,--Webster of the class of 1833, sealed his faith with his life on the bloody field of the second Manassas, dying for the constitution of which his great father was the noblest expounder. For those of us who return to-day, whatever our perils and dangers may have been, we can not feel that we have done enough to merit what you so generously bestow; but for those with whom the work of this life is finished and yet who live forever inseparably linked with the great names of the founders of the Republic, and not them alone, but the heroes and martyrs of liberty everywhere, we know that no honor can be too much. The voices which rang out so loud and clear upon the charging cheer that heralded the final assault in the hour of victory, that in the hour of disaster were so calm and resolute as they sternly struggled to stay the slow retreat are not silent yet. To us and to those who will come after us, they will speak of comfort and home relinquished, of toil nobly borne, of danger manfully encountered, of life generously surrendered and this not for pelf or ambition, but in the spirit of the noblest self-devotion and the most exalted patriotism. Proud as we who are here to-day have a right to be that we are the sons of this university, and not deemed unworthy of her when these are remembered, we may well say, "Sparta had many a worthier son than we."

FOOTNOTE:

[10] Speech at Commemoration Exercises held at Cambridge, July 21, 1865.

WAKE UP, ENGLAND![11]

BY KING GEORGE

In the name of the Queen and the other members of my family, on behalf of the Princess and for myself, I thank you most sincerely for your enthusiastic reception of this toast, proposed by you, my Lord Mayor, in such kind and generous terms. Your feeling allusion to our recent long absence from our happy family circle gives expression to that sympathy which has been so universally extended to my dear parents, whether in times of joy or sorrow, by the people of this country, and upon which my dear mother felt she could ever reckon from the first days of her life here amongst them. As to ourselves, we are deeply sensible of the great honor done us on this occasion, and our hearts are moved by the splendid reception which to-day has been accorded us by the authorities and inhabitants of the City of London. And I desire to take this opportunity to express our deepest gratitude for the sympathetic interest with which our journey was followed by our fellow countrymen at home, and for the warm welcome with which we were greeted on our return. You were good enough, my Lord Mayor, to refer to his Majesty having marked our home-coming by creating me Prince of Wales. I only hope that I may be worthy to hold that ancient and historic title, which was borne by my dear father for upward of fifty-nine years.

My Lord Mayor, you have attributed to us more credit than I think we deserve. For I feel that the debt of gratitude is not the nation's to us, but ours to the King and Government for having made it possible for us to carry out, with every consideration for our comfort and convenience, a voyage unique in its character, rich in the experience gained and in memories of warm and affectionate greetings from the many races of his Majesty's subjects in his great dominions beyond the seas. And here in the capital of our great Empire I would repeat how profoundly touched and gratified we have been by the loyalty, affection and enthusiasm which invariably characterized the welcome extended to us throughout our long and memorable tour. It may interest you to know that we travelled over 45,000 miles, of which 33,000 were by sea, and I think it is a matter of which all may feel proud that, with the exception of Port Said, we never set foot on any land where the Union Jack did not fly. Leaving England in the middle of March, we first touched at Gibraltar and Malta, where, as a sailor, I was proud to meet the two great fleets of the Channel and Mediterranean. Passing through the Suez Canal--a monument of the genius and courage of a gifted son of the great friendly nation across the Channel--we entered at Aden the gateway of the East. We stayed for a short time to enjoy the unrivaled scenery of Ceylon and the Malay Peninsula, the gorgeous displays of their native races, and to see in what happy contentment these various peoples live and prosper under British rule. Perhaps there was something still more striking in the fact that the Government, the commerce, and every form of enterprise in these countries are under the leadership and direction of but a handful of our countrymen, and to realize the high qualities of the men who have won and kept for us that splendid condition. Australia saw the consummation of the great mission which was the more immediate object of our journey, and you can imagine the feelings of pride with which I presided over the inauguration of the first representative Assembly of the new-born Australian Commonwealth, in whose hands are placed the destinies of the great island continent. During a happy stay of many weeks in the different States, we were able to gain an insight into the working of the commercial, social and political institutions of which the country justly boasts, and to see something of the great progress which it has already made, and of its great capabilities, while making the acquaintance of the warm-hearted and large-minded men to whose personality and energy so much of that progress is due. New Zealand afforded us a striking example of a vigorous, independent and prosperous people, living in the full enjoyment of free and liberal institutions, and where many interesting social experiments are being put to the test of experience. Here we had the satisfaction of meeting large gatherings of the Maori people--once a brave and resolute foe, now peaceful and devoted subjects of the King. Tasmania, which in natural characteristics and climate reminded us of the old country, was visited when our faces were at length turned homeward. Mauritius, with its beautiful tropical scenery, its classical, literary and naval historical associations, and its population gifted with all the charming characteristics of old France, was our first halting-place, on our way to receive, in Natal and Cape Colony, a welcome remarkable in its warmth and enthusiasm, which appeared to be accentuated by the heavy trial of the long and grievous war under which they have suffered. To Canada was borne the message--already conveyed to Australia and New Zealand--of the Motherland's loving appreciation of the services rendered by her gallant sons. In a journey from ocean to ocean, marvelous in its comfort and organization, we were enabled to see something of its matchless scenery, the richness of its soil, the boundless possibilities of that vast and but partly explored territory. We saw, too, the success which has crowned the efforts to weld into one community the peoples of its two great races. Our final halting-place was, by the express desire of the King, Newfoundland, the oldest of our colonies and the first visited by his Majesty in 1860. The hearty seafaring population of this island gave us a reception the cordiality of which is still fresh in our memories.

If I were asked to specify any particular impressions derived from our journey, I should unhesitatingly place before all others that of loyalty to the

Crown and of attachment to the country; and it was touching to hear the invariable reference to home, even from the lips of those who never had been or were never likely to be in these islands. And with this loyalty were unmistakable evidences of the consciousness of strength; of a true and living membership in the Empire, and of power and readiness to share the burden and responsibility of that membership. And were I to seek for the causes which have created and fostered this spirit, I should venture to attribute them, in a very large degree, to the light and example of our late beloved Sovereign. It would be difficult to exaggerate the signs of genuine sorrow for her loss and of love for her memory which we found among all races, even in the most remote districts which we visited. Besides this, may we not find another cause--the wise and just policy which in the last half century has been continuously maintained toward our colonies? As a result of the happy relations thus created between the mother country and her colonies we have seen their spontaneous rally round the old flag in defense of the nation's honor in South Africa. I had ample opportunities to form some estimate of the military strength of Australia, New Zealand, and Canada, having reviewed upward of 60,000 troops. Abundant and excellent material is available, requiring only that molding into shape which can be readily effected by the hands of capable and experienced officers. I am anxious to refer to an admirable movement which has taken strong root in both Australia and New Zealand--and that is the cadet corps. On several occasions I had the gratification of seeing march past several thousand cadets, armed and equipped, and who at the expense of their respective Governments are able to go through a military course, and in some cases with an annual grant of practise ammunition. I will not presume, in these days of army reform, to do more than call the attention of my friend, the Secretary of State for War, to this interesting fact.

To the distinguished representatives of the commercial interests of the Empire, whom I have the pleasure of seeing here to-day, I venture to allude to the impression which seemed generally to prevail among their brethren across the seas, that the old country must wake up if she intends to maintain her old position of pre-eminence in her colonial trade against foreign competitors. No one who had the privilege of enjoying the experiences which we have had during our tour could fail to be struck with one all-prevailing and pressing demand: the want of population. Even in the oldest of our colonies there were abundant signs of this need. Boundless tracts of country yet unexplored, hidden mineral wealth calling for development, vast expanses of virgin soil ready to yield profitable crops to the settlers. And these can be enjoyed under conditions of healthy living, liberal laws, free institutions, in exchange for the over-crowded cities and the almost hopeless struggle for existence which, alas, too often is the lot of many in the old country. But one condition, and one only, is made by our colonial brethren, and that is, "Send us suitable emigrants." I would go further, and appeal to my fellow countrymen at home to prove the strength of the attachment of the motherland to her children by sending to them only of her best. By this means we may still further strengthen, or at all events pass on unimpaired, that pride of race, that unity of sentiment and purpose, that feeling of common loyalty and obligation which knit together and alone can maintain the integrity of our Empire.

FOOTNOTE:

[11] A speech delivered by His Majesty King George when Prince of Wales, at the Guildhall, London, December 5, 1901, on his return from his tour of the Empire. With the permission of the proprietors of The Times the report which appeared in that paper has been followed.

www.ingramcontent.com/pod-product-compliance
Lightning Source LLC
Chambersburg PA
CBHW070916180526
45168CB00005B/2040